Australian
Language & Culture

Australian Language & Culture
3rd edition – March 2007
First published – October 1994

Published by
Lonely Planet Publications Pty Ltd ABN 36 005 607 983
90 Maribyrnong St, Footscray, Victoria 3011, Australia

Lonely Planet Offices
Australia Locked Bag 1, Footscray, Victoria 3011
USA 150 Linden St, Oakland CA 94607
UK 72–82 Rosebery Ave, London, EC1R 4RW

Cover
Australian montage by Yukiyoshi Kamimura
© Lonely Planet Publications Pty Ltd 2007

ISBN 978 1 74059 099 0

10 9 8 7 6 5 4 3 2

Printed by C&C Offset Printing Co Ltd, China

ACKNOWLEDGMENTS

Editor Vanessa Battersby would like to acknowledge the following people for their contributions to this phrasebook:

Paul Smitz for updating the Australian English section. Paul is a native of Australia (despite some vague Belgian lineage, something to do with his parents apparently) and has had many years to practice muttering thin-lipped colloquialisms and verbally cut down tall poppies. Paul would like to thank Vanessa Battersby for her fine editorial work, Ben Handicott for getting it all started, and Karin Vidstrup Monk for just being Karin. He'd also like to thank all the people he eavesdropped on while conducting his 'research'.

Barry Blake for updating the Australian Aboriginal language section. Barry, who retired from the chair of linguistics at La Trobe University in 2003, has been studying Australian languages since 1966 when he began work on several languages of western Queensland. Recently he has produced a number of descriptions of the languages of Victoria based on 19th-century sources.

Elizabeth Swan, editor, and authors Denise Angelo, Peter Austin, Susan Butler, Carolyn Coleman, Jane Curtain, Alan Dench, Mark Newbrook, Dana Ober, Jenny Tindale, Melanie Wilkinson and many others for their work on the earlier editions upon which this book was based. Thanks also to Mike McDermott and Michael Hanrahan for their input on the Sport chapter.

Lonely Planet Language Products

Publishing Manager: Chris Rennie

Commissioning Editors: Karin Vidstrup Monk & Ben Handicott

Editor: Vanessa Battersby

Assisting Editor: Branislava Vladisavljevic

Layout Designer: Yukiyoshi Kamimura

Cartographer: Wayne Murphy

Project Manager & Managing Editor: Annelies Mertens

Layout Manager: Kate McDonald

Series Designer: Yukiyoshi Kamimura

CONTENTS

4

Australia's states and territories

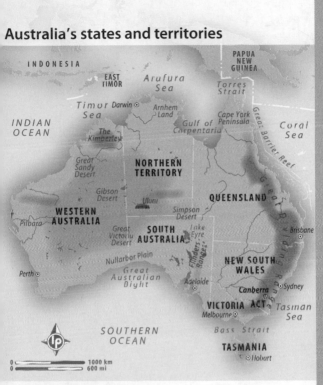

Australian states & territories

Australia consists of six states and two territories:

New South Wales	**NSW**
Queensland	**QLD**
South Australia	**SA**
Tasmania	**TAS**
Victoria	**VIC**
Western Australia	**WA**
Australian Capital Territory	**ACT**
Northern Territory	**NT**

When the British government established a convict settlement in Sydney Cove in 1788 they wouldn't even have thought about the linguistic consequences. The history of Australian English is not just one of transplantation from the UK to Australia, within the dour confines of the First Fleet, but also of adaptation. As time went by, both the convicts and the free settlers adapted English to their new home, twisting the meanings of existing words and borrowing new ones to suit.

The beginnings of Australian English

CONVICT INFLUENCE

The earliest Australian English was very much a working-class variety, as the vast majority of the UK arrivals (mostly convicts) were poor and unskilled. Some words even filtered through from what was called the 'Flash Language' – the thieves' language of London – which earned an unexpected respectability on Australian shores. For example, in London 'plant' was the name for stolen goods hidden away to be collected later when it was safe. In early Australian English the word came to refer to stores and provisions hidden away in the bush to be collected on a return trip, and a matching verb 'to plant' was created. So when contemporary Australians speak of *planting* Christmas presents where the children can't find them, they're using old British criminal slang.

EARLY BRITISH ENGLISH INFLUENCE

Words and expressions from British English took on a whole new meaning in colonial Australia. For example, in the UK a 'paddock' is a small enclosed meadow – in Australia a 'paddock' may extend further than the eye can see. In the UK a 'creek' is a small tidal inlet – in Australia a 'creek' is a subsidiary of a river and can be bigger than the Thames.

Australian English is predominantly a town-based language, as most of the convicts and early settlers were from British towns and cities, especially London and communities in the southeast of England. This partially explains why rural British English labels such as 'brook', 'glen' and 'dale' haven't become part of the Australian English vocabulary.

BUSHRANGING

Bushranging is the robbery of settlers by thieves (*bushrangers*) who hide in the Australian bush. Ned Kelly (1855–80) is the most famous and iconic bushranger, and lives on in the Australian imagination as the personification of some prized characteristics: bravery, cheekiness and compassion for fellow battlers.

Ned led colonial authorities a merry dance for years, and his downfall only came about after he and his gang (which consisted mainly of his brothers) had held up the entire town of Glenrowan in Victoria. The Melbourne establishment sent out a trainload of police and trackers, but Ned organised *fettlers* (railway workers) to dig up the tracks and derail the train. Unfortunately for the gang, the Glenrowan schoolmaster escaped and managed to stop the train in time. The bushrangers donned home-made armour for the resultant shoot-out but were outnumbered, and only Ned survived to stand trial in Melbourne. His last words before he was hanged were said to be 'Such is life'.

Other bushrangers worth a mention include Captain Moonlite and Captain Thunderbolt, who were good bushmen and rather elegant performers on the thievery stage. Brave Ben Hall was not so much a sinner as a man sinned against – he took to *bushranging* because of basic injustice. Mad Dog Morgan, on the other hand, was noted for his brutality.

EARLY IRISH ENGLISH INFLUENCE

The other main influence on Australian English was Irish English, as convicts were also transported from Ireland following the 1798 Irish rebellion. Later on, in the 1840s, many Irish migrants were forced to settle in Australia after the potato famine. Australian English has therefore incorporated a number of Irish English words and phrases into its vocabulary. The term *sheila*, for example, is an Irish girls' name which was used in early Australian English to apply to any Irish girl, just as *paddy* was used for any Irish man. Later on *sheila* began to be used for any woman, although it's not a term women have typically applied to themselves. In colloquial Australian English it also became a derogatory label for a man who was considered to 'behave like a woman', and is still wielded in this way by certain (sexist) Aussie males!

Irish English has also had some influence on Australian English grammar (see page 24).

THE GOLDFIELDS

The gold fever that began afflicting prospectors in the 1850s led to an influx of people from all over the world, including the UK, Ireland, elsewhere in Europe, North America and Asia. Many British and American slang and colloquial expressions came to Australia during this period. Some words still survive from the diggings era – words like *fossick,* which used to mean 'dig through a heap of dirt for any leftover gold' and now means 'go carefully through anything in order to find something'. The word *digger* is another import from the gold rushes. It then referred to a miner, but since miners for safety reasons always worked in pairs, the *digger* became the symbol of mateship in Australia, particularly during the hardships of the world wars.

FOOL'S GOLD

There's a story that *dinkum* (which means 'honest' or 'genuine', as do the expressions *fair dinkum* and *dinky-di*) is a Chinese word meaning 'real gold' and dates from the goldfields era, when distinguishing real gold from false was an issue, but this is apparently folklore. For a more popular etymology of *dinkum*, see page 42.

20th-century Australian English

The Federation of the Australian States, which was formed on 1 January 1901, was a watershed in Australian history and separates the former colonial society from the modern nation. Subsequently, there were a number of significant additions to Australian English.

In World War I, soldiers contributed some slang such as *furphy* (rumour). During the war, water was supplied to the soldiers in water carts made by John Furphy. The obvious place for the soldiers to exchange information of doubtful value was at the water cart, so these rumours came to be called *furphies*.

During the Great Depression the figure of the *battler* emerged (a person who struggles against all odds). The *battler* was usually surviving on the *susso* (sustenance payments). These days you'll often hear the rather simplistic phrase 'little Aussie battler' used to describe any Australian who lacks money and other resources but continues to slug it out with that ogre Life regardless.

World War II sparked an influx of Americanisms along with terms from army talk like *troppo* (mad from spending too much time in the tropics) and *spine-bashing* (resting).

Since the 1950s in particular, Australia has received a significant number of migrants who speak a language other than English at home. Their English is often, of course, influenced by their other language, but there's not a lot of evidence that this has spread to the wider population.

Recent history

Australian English has been particularly influenced by American English over the last half-century. Although its English-speaking immigrants have mainly come from the UK, Australia's close ties with the USA and the worldwide influence of American music and movies have led to noticeable Americanisation. Australian kids appear to still use 'biscuit' rather than the American word 'cookie' and pronounce the letter z to rhyme with 'head' rather than with 'bee', but they readily refer to other people as 'guys' and 'chicks' and when something excites them are apt to call it 'awesome'.

As well as this Americanisation, Australian English is subject to the homogenising influence of nationwide television, movies and radio. Nevertheless, there are still differences between country and city speech, with country people tending to sound 'broader' and more colloquial.

Another noticeable pattern is the growing difference between the language used by older and younger generations. Much of the colloquial language that's regarded as distinctively Australian now tends to be used more by older people.

Borrowings

ABORIGINAL BORROWINGS

There aren't many words in Australian English that are borrowed from Aboriginal languages, but they often identify significant cultural items. The pattern of borrowing pretty much follows the precedent set by Captain Cook with **kangaroo** – words are only borrowed for totally new items. To European eyes the kangaroo was an extraordinary animal, quite unlike anything they'd ever come across before. Many other plants and animals could be named a native this or that – the koala, for example, was originally called a 'native bear' and the angophora was called the 'native apple' – but a kangaroo couldn't be thought of as a native anything.

So, Cook asked the people of the Guugu Yimidhirr tribe of North Queensland what they called the animal, noted *kangaroo* in his diary, and thus the first major borrowing came about.

There's a curious sequel to this story. Relations between indigenous people and Europeans in Australia went from bad to worse, so that after the first great influx of Aboriginal words in the colonial period there was no traffic between Aboriginal languages and Australian English. So, when people finally became interested enough to attempt to track down the origin of *kangaroo*, they couldn't locate the word in local languages. They were possibly thrown off by the fact that whereas in English the difference between *k* and *g* is significant, in the language of the Guugu Yimidhirr there's no distinction between the two. In any case, a rumour developed that in fact Cook had been hoodwinked by the Aborigines and that the word *kangaroo* meant either 'I don't know' or something very rude. The misunderstanding has since been resolved – *kangaroo* means 'kangaroo' in anyone's language – but the folklore persists.

The words that have been borrowed are generally the names of animals and plants. They come from a number of different Aboriginal languages, depending on where the Europeans turned up, with the largest number of borrowings coming from the languages of the eastern coast. Following are some examples, divided into regions.

The Brisbane region

barramundi	fish
dilly	bag made of twisted grass or fibre
yakka	work

HARD YAKKA

Yakka is a popular brand of work clothes worn by labourers, electricians (*sparkies*), carpenters (*chippies*), plumbers and other construction workers. It's obligatory to complete the outfit with a pair of *Blunnies* – Blundstone boots.

Inland New South Wales

billabong	waterhole
brigalow	tree
brolga	bird
budgerigar	small, brightly coloured bird
coolamon	wooden dish
gidgee	type of tree
quandong	type of tree with edible fruit
yarraman	horse

Inland Victoria

mallee	tree
mia-mia	rough shelter
mulga	type of wattle

Northern Queensland

cooee	cry made to signal one's presence in the bush
kangaroo	kangaroo

The Outback

coolibah	species of tree
didgeridoo	long wooden musical wind instrument
nardoo	kind of fern

The Perth region

bardy	edible grub
euro	wallaby
jarrah	species of large eucalypt
karri	species of eucalypt
kylie	boomerang
marron	crayfish
quokka	small wallaby
wandoo	type of eucalypt
wongi	to talk

Southern South Australia

joey	baby kangaroo
willy-willy	sudden circling gust of wind
wurley	rough shelter

Southern Victoria

belah	tree
bingie	stomach or belly
luderick	fish
yabba	talk

The Sydney region

bogie	swimming hole
bombora	current over a submerged reef
boobook	small owl or mopoke
boomerang	curved piece of wood used as a missile
bettong	rat-kangaroo
corella	large parrot, predominantly white with pink or orange-red markings
corroboree	Aboriginal ceremony
currawong	large black-and-white bird with yellow eyes and a loud ringing call

dingo	native dog
geebung	small tree
gibber	rock or stone
gunyah	rough shelter or dwelling
koala	'bear-like' marsupial
kurrajong	tree
myall	wild (from an Aboriginal word meaning 'stranger')
nulla-nulla	Aboriginal club or weapon
pademelon	wallaby
potoroo	small wallaby
wallaby	small cousin of the kangaroo
waratah	flower with large showy red petals, the emblem of NSW
warrigal	dingo
wombat	nocturnal marsupial the size of a small pig which lives in a burrow
woomera	Aboriginal weapon

PLACE NAMES

Aboriginal words and their meanings were also appropriated for Australian English place names, including the following:

Allora	waterhole; a town in Queensland
Amaroo	beautiful place, red mud or rain; a town in New South Wales
Babinda	waterfall; a town in Queensland
Dandenong	lofty mountain; a mountain range in Victoria
Dorrigo	stringybark; a town in New South Wales
Dunedoo	swan; a town in New South Wales
Ekibin	a part of the river where indigenous people could obtain edible aquatic roots; a place in Brisbane
Murrumbidgee	big water; a river in New South Wales
Narooma	blue water; a town in New South Wales
Ulladulla	safe harbour; a coastal town in New South Wales
Wagga Wagga	crows; a town in New South Wales
Waikerie	wings or anything that flies; a town in South Australia

A few place names were borrowed from Aboriginal mythology:

Arkaroola town in the northern Flinders Ranges in South Australia. Named after a great Dreamtime snake, Arkaroo, which drank Lake Frome dry and carved out the bed of the Arkaroola Creek.

Gidgealpa town in South Australia. The word's meaning is 'to stand in the shade of a grey rain cloud', a reference to Kilyalpani, one of the mythical women who created the land. It was said that once, while she was praying for rain, a grey cloud formed above her.

In the 1990s, after decades of no borrowings, some new Aboriginal words began to be added to Australian English. A notable one is *Koori*, a word from the Awakabal tribe near Newcastle, just north of Sydney. *Koori* has been used by some

Aborigines to refer to an Aborigine of eastern Australia since the early part of last century.

Place names have also started being borrowed again, beginning with the reinstatement of the Loritdja word for that great red monolith in Central Australia, **Uluru** (formerly known as Ayers Rock). Similarly, the nearby Olgas are now once again **Kata Tjuta** and Kings Canyon is **Watarrka**.

MYTHICAL LANGUAGE

A small set of Aboriginal words are entrenched in the national folklore. What would the Australian dreamscape be without the **bunyip**, a mythical creature that lives in waterholes and is thought to cause loud noises at night and (rather more terrifyingly) devour women and children? The **bunyip** comes to us from Wemba Wemba, a language of western Victoria, and was subject to an interesting description in 1847 in the newspaper *Bell's Life in Sydney*: 'That apochryphal animal of many names, commonly designated The Bunyip has, according to a correspondent of *The Sydney Morning Herald*, been seen on the Murrumbidgee. It's described as being about as big as a six months old calf, of dark brown colour, a long neck, a long pointed head, large ears, a thick mane of hair from the head down the neck, and two large tusks. It's said to be an amphibious animal, as it has been observed floundering in the rivers, as well as grazing on their banks.'

Mythologically speaking, waterholes appear to be extremely dangerous places as they're also plagued by a hairy snake called the **mindi**. Watch out for the **yowie**, too, a huge ape-like monster from the stories of the Yuwaalaraay of northern New South Wales – the Aboriginal word translates as 'dream spirit'. On the plains of northern Queensland, you should also beware of the **min-min** light, a will-o'-the-wisp which is regarded as an evil apparition.

AMERICAN BORROWINGS

As already mentioned, the basic British influence in Australian English has been overlaid since World War II by a strong US flavour. Among the US items which made it into Australian English over the past two decades are:

bag lady   an elderly woman who's homeless and who carries all her belongings in a shopping bag

cockamamie   crazy; ridiculous; all muddled up

cornball   sentimentalist given to trite and hackneyed sayings

deep throat   anonymous informant within an organisation who leaks information to an outsider. In May 2005 the original Deep Throat, of Watergate fame, finally revealed himself as former FBI deputy director Mark Felt.

d'oh   expression made famous by Homer Simpson, meant to indicate that you're reprimanding yourself for some new piece of stupidity

dork   someone who's socially clumsy, dresses badly and generally makes an idiot of himself/herself. Used in place of the Australian word *dag*.

fast track   make something happen unusually quickly

life in the fast lane   this is 1980s talk. At the height of 'yuppiedom' life in the fast lane was 'where it was at'.

mover and shaker   important and influential person who makes things happen

parlay   to convert a sum of money into an even larger sum by taking a gamble with it

psychobabble   the jargon of psychology, particularly that used in psychotherapy groups

spin doctor   person who runs media campaigns for a company or politician, and specialises in putting a positive 'spin' on news through selective emphasis and obfuscation, if not outright distortion, of the truth

(a) tad a little. There's a theory that it's a shortening of 'tadpole' as applied to a small child (also used in parts of England).

underclass the category of impoverished people who fall outside society's safety nets and have a lifestyle, culture and set of values at odds with mainstream society

wimp weak, effeminate, cowardly person. To be too afraid to do something is known as *wimping out*. This word is being overtaken by *wuss* or *wussy* but is still popular.

UK BORROWINGS

Australian English hasn't lost touch with the UK entirely. Many items of British English still find their way into Australian English. For example:

aggro aggressive, as in 'Don't be so aggro.' The Australian use is slightly different from the British one – Australians don't really talk about 'giving people aggro', they tend to just say someone 'was aggro'.

gobsmacked astonished. The image that lurks behind this word is the reflex action of the hand covering the open mouth (*gob*) after an enormous shock.

minder bequeathed by the popular 1980s television program *Minder*, in which it meant 'a criminal's bodyguard' – the word now applies to anyone whose job it is to shield someone else from unpleasantness (pop stars have minders, as do politicians)

ALL MIXED UP

Australia has taken a pick'n'mix approach to British and American terms. For example, Australia has *trucks* (an American word) and *truckies* rather than *lorries* and *lorry drivers* (British), but they visit *petrol stations* (British) rather than *gas stations* (American).

Being informal and speaking informally is an important part of Australian culture, and slang and colloquial language are a normal part of Australian English – though of course Australians can be as formal as anyone else when it's appropriate. It's thought this informality is partly due to the fact that most of the first English-speaking settlers in Australia were convicted criminals. In any case, for many Australians, being informal expresses desired values of equality and solidarity. Australians often portray their country as classless, and while this is not entirely true, it's certainly a lot less class-conscious than, say, the UK.

Pronunciation

Very early in the days of colonial settlement, British visitors were prone to commenting (usually disparagingly) on the Australian accent. Various attempts were made to correct the 'twisted vowels' and 'barbaric noises' made by the locals from that early point in colonial history until comparatively recently. But the accent that formed among the descendants of the convicts and settlers has proven remarkably resistant to such efforts. There are two main theories on how the Aussie twang came about – the 'melting pot' theory and the 'stranded dialect' theory.

THE MELTING POT THEORY

The early convict settlements included speakers of various British dialects, whose accents remained much as they were before they landed on Australian shores. Being transported didn't change a Yorkshireman into something else, and there was no way that a Cockney convict was going to start imitating his military masters. But the children of the convicts were like children anywhere – eager to conform and win the acceptance of the other children. So, the theory is that with no one particular local form of language to guide them, they forged a new accent of their own by blending the various accents represented among them.

THE STRANDED DIALECT THEORY

The melting pot theory does seem to have a lot going for it, but there's an alternative – that there was a predominant dialect among the convict community which became the Australian English of today, but that this dialect is difficult to trace back to its British origins for two reasons. Firstly, although there's a conservative force operating in a colony that resists change, that force doesn't operate back in the mother country, where the dialect continues to change. So, the older form is stranded in the colony.

Secondly, circumstances may have forced changes on the colonial speakers which confused the issue, making it harder to decide just what the original home accent was. The presence of a large group of speakers with one accent, for example, might bring about changes in the speech of the rest of the community simply through the pressure of numbers.

We can't know for sure which (if any) of the theories is right. Perhaps both are partly valid.

THE INFLUENCE OF US PRONUNCIATION

Although American English has had an obvious influence on Australian vocabulary (and on some areas of grammar), very few words show any American influence on their pronunciation. It's said that the only time Australians actually sound American is when they're crooning popular songs – a vocal crutch shared by pop singers from other English-speaking communities. However, this too may be changing, as more Australian musicians seem to be singing in their normal accents.

DIFFERENCES ACROSS AUSTRALIA

Australian English is remarkably homogeneous, despite the fact that it's over 3000km from the west coast to the east.

Most speakers sound the same or very similar, and there are no big regional differences compared to the UK or the USA. The main geographical difference is thought to be the city versus country divide – the rural accent is supposedly slower and broader than the urban.

Still, there is some evidence that subtle differences in pronunciation between regions do exist. For example, many people in Melbourne, Brisbane and Hobart use the short *a* vowel (as in 'cat') in words like 'castle', 'graph' and 'dance', while the long *a* (as in 'cart') is normally used in other parts of Australia. Similarly, in South Australia and parts of Victoria the word 'school' and others like it tend to be pronounced with a clipped, shortened vowel not common elsewhere. Some linguists believe these sorts of changes are becoming more noticeable. (For more on differences in speech across Australia, see page 125.)

One distinctive pattern that emerged among young people over the past few decades, but now seems to be in decline, was the use of rising intonation – statements like 'That's my favourite film' would have the rising pitch which is usually reserved for questions. It has been mercilessly lampooned in Australian television and film, which may be one reason it's in decline.

BATMANIA

Rumour has it that Melbourne narrowly escaped being named 'Batmania' in honour of John Batman, who selected the city's site in 1835. But even without 'Batmania', Australia still has its fair share of places with strange names. Some intriguing ones include:

Bald Head (WA)	*Indented Head (Vic)*
Banana (Qld)	*Lake Disappointment (WA)*
Big Billy Bore (Vic)	*Mexican Hat Beach (WA)*
Booby Island (Qld)	*Mt Hopeless (SA)*
Broken Bucket Reserve (Vic)	*Nightcap (NSW)*
Butty Head (WA)	*One Arm Point (Vic)*
Cape Liptrap (Vic)	*Salmon Gums (WA)*
Humpty Doo (NT)	*Snug (Tas)*

Grammar

There aren't many grammatical features exclusive to Australian English, but the ones that exist can sometimes cause a little confusion for visitors.

all/both ... not   when younger Australians say things like 'All those letters didn't arrive', they usually mean 'None of those letters arrived.' Older Australians don't often use such sentences, but if they do they put the stress on 'all' and the sentence then means 'Some of them arrived and some didn't.' Just to add a bit of excitement to the day, some people use both meanings.

as such ...   young Australians sometimes use 'as such' in cases where 'so', 'therefore', or a similar expression would be usual elsewhere: 'The building's locked; as such, we can't get our things.'

as well ...   like Canadians (but not like most Americans or British), Australians sometimes begin sentences with 'As well ...' as in 'As well, there are three other problems.'

conditionals   in Australia, the phrase 'If that happened ...' doesn't always mean that the speaker thinks the event in question might happen (but probably won't) in the future, as in 'If that happened tomorrow I'd be surprised.' It sometimes means that it *could* have happened in the past but didn't, as in 'If that happened yesterday I'd have been surprised.' Most people from other English-speaking countries would say 'If that had happened ...' or, in the USA, 'If that would have happened ...'

different to the majority of Australians use 'to' after 'different', as in 'Adelaide is very different to Perth.' Some older people and most formal writings still use the more typically British word 'from'. However, the originally American form, 'than', is becoming increasingly popular.

hottest, highest, etc when an Australian news report says that yesterday was the hottest May day since 1927, it doesn't imply – as it might elsewhere – that the day in May 1927 was even hotter, it implies that it was the same temperature. This can be very confusing at first for people addicted to weather or statistic-laden sport reports.

irregardless this word is a blend of 'irrespective' and 'regardless' and has the same meaning ('Irregardless of what you think, I'm going to do it!'). It's heard elsewhere but seems to be especially common in Australia.

may & might if an Australian says something like 'Bruce may have sung', sometimes the singing referred to *could* have happened but didn't. Most non-Australians would use 'might', not 'may', in this case. Using 'may' would normally mean that they don't know whether it happened or not. Australians also often say things like 'Pete said that Bruce may sing', even where the singing predicted by Pete would be in the past if it had happened. Again, 'might' would be more usual elsewhere.

mustn't as in Ireland and parts of England, Australian English uses the word 'mustn't'. Many Australians say things like 'She mustn't be in – the lights are all out.' In most other English-speaking countries people would say 'She can't be in' or, in the USA, 'She must not be in.'

my same some Australians say things like 'Can I keep my same phone number if I change address?' In the majority of other English-speaking countries the expression in such cases is always 'the same'.

usedn't to for most English speakers, the negative of 'used to' is 'didn't use to', as in 'I didn't use to like beer but now I do.' The older form 'usedn't to' ('I usedn't to like beer …') is now rare, but Australia is one of its remaining habitats.

verbs used with team names   in Australia, as in America, the names of sports teams can be either singular or plural. So people may say either 'West Coast (the football team) is doing well' or 'West Coast are doing well.' In the UK, by contrast, team names are always plural ('Liverpool are doing well'). Although it's less common, Australians also use singular nouns and pronouns to refer to teams occasionally. So in an Australian newspaper, a sentence like 'It's the reigning champion' could refer to a football team.

youse   pronounced 'yooz', this has become the plural of 'you'. You may hear sentences like 'Where are youse going?' Only used by the grammatically challenged.

> ## YEAH NO
>
> In the past, if an Australian paused or hesitated before answering a question asked, they'd often fill the gap with an 'um' – in the case of the more ponderous talker, extended to the length of a monk's meditative chant. But nowadays the humble 'um' seems to have yielded to the contradictory, self-cancelling and terribly addictive 'yeah no'. It's common, for instance, to hear media interviewees (particularly sports-people) begin their answer to a journalist's question with a firm 'yeah no'. Some linguists believe that 'yeah no' acts as more than just a gap-filler, and is a way of politely accepting and then downplaying or questioning a compliment or assertion.

Shortened forms

Australians are fond of cutting their words down to size, usually by taking the first part of the word and finishing it off with *-ie* or *-o*. This can be used to indicate affection, especially on names but also on ordinary words – children, for example, are sometimes referred to as ***kiddies***, or even more playfully, ***kiddiewinks***. The *-ie* ending is also used to create useful new nouns from adjectives – like the word ***greenie*** (person concerned about the environment) from *green*. The *-o* ending is a bit more neutral than the *-ie* one and can be used to convey a certain nonchalance.

There's a school of thought that says the Australian addiction to abbreviation, with all its informality, is due to a middle-class desire to appear down to earth despite craving an upper-class standard of living – in other words, people want to live like the elite but can't stand to think of themselves as elitist.

Note that it's not unusual to find words ending in *-ie* also spelled with a *-y* ending. Thus *cabbie* could well be spelled *cabby*. However, for some inscrutable reason various words always take *-ie* and others always take *-y*. In the same way, some words can take *-o* as well as *-ie* or *-y*, but some only take *-o*. Here are some of the more common *-ie* words:

Aussie	Australian
barbie	barbecue
bickie	biscuit – 'big bickies' means a lot of money
bikie	motorbike rider
Blunnies	Blundstone workboots
bookie	bookmaker at sporting events
brekkie	breakfast
brickie	bricklayer
Brizzie	Brisbane
cabbie	cab/taxi driver
cardie	cardigan
chippie	carpenter
chockie	chocolate
Chrissie	Christmas
ciggie	cigarette
conchie	conscientious person, or conscientious objector
druggie	drug addict
flattie	flathead (fish), or flat tyre
foodie	a gourmet
freebie	something for free
goalie	goalkeeper
goodies	treats
hottie	hot-water bottle

jarmies	pyjamas
leckie	electric blanket
lippie	lipstick
littlie	little thing, or child
meanie	mean person
newie	new item
oldie	old item, or your parents (when in the plural)
pokie	poker machine
pollie	politician
possie	position (pronounced 'pozzie')
postie	mail deliverer
prezzie	present
prozzie	prostitute
rellie	a relative

rollie	'roll-your-own' cigarette
sickie	day off sick (or supposedly sick)
smoothie	smooth talker, or drink made with blended fruit
sparkie	electrician
subbie	subcontractor
sunnies	sunglasses
swiftie	a trick – *to pull a swiftie* is to trick someone
taddie	tadpole
Tassie	Tasmania (pronounced 'tazzie')
tinnie	can of beer
trannie	transistor radio, or transvestite
truckie	truckdriver
U-ie	U-turn in a car (pronounced 'yoowee')
umpie	umpire
undies	underpants
wharfie	a wharf labourer
Windies	the West Indian cricket team
Woolies	Woolworths (supermarket chain)
woollies	woollen clothes

A WEIRDIE

According to *The Story of English* (Penguin Books, 1986), well-known Aussie performer Barry Humphries claimed he once heard an Australian woman describing her hospital visit for a hysterectomy as 'having a *hizzie* in the *hozzie*'.

A few words that nearly always use the *-y* spelling include:

Bundy	Bundaberg rum, or Bundaberg (a town)
comfy	comfortable
divvy van	police divisional van
dunny	toilet
exy	expensive
footy	football
kindy	kindergarten
placky	plastic
Rocky	Rockhampton
stubby	bottle of beer
telly	TV

The following always take *-o*:

ammo	ammunition
arvo	afternoon
avo	avocado
combo	combination
compo	compensation
demo	demonstration
dero	derelict person
doco	documentary
Freo	Fremantle
garbo	garbage collector
gyno	gynaecologist
info	information
intro	introduction
journo	journalist
kero	kerosene

metho	methylated spirits
milko	milk deliverer
muso	musician
porno	pornography, or pornographic
rego	car registration
Salvo	Salvation Army member
servo	petrol station
smoko	break for a cigarette
speedo	speedometer
vego	vegetarian person or meal (pronounced 'vejo')
wino	an alcoholic who drinks cheap wine

CHOOKS, CROCS & COCKIES

Given their penchant for shortening existing words and inventing new ones, it'll come as no surprise that Australians have given their friends (and foes) in the animal world a few 'special' names:

barra	barramundi (fish)
bitie	biting insect
blowie	blowfly
bluey	blue heeler dog
boomer	large kangaroo
brumby	wild horse
budgie	budgerigar
bug	small crustacean, as in 'Moreton Bay bug'
bushman's clock	kookaburra
chook	chicken
cocky	cockatoo, or cockroach
croc	crocodile
dunny budgie	fly
freshie	freshwater crocodile
maggie	magpie
mozzie	mosquito
muddie	mud crab
roo	kangaroo
saltie	saltwater crocodile
sandie	sand crab
stinger	stinging jellyfish, especially box jellyfish
yabby	small freshwater crayfish

NAMES

Many famous Australians are affectionately known by versions of their first names or surnames ending in -ie, -o or -y. So cricketer Shane Warne is called 'Warnie', and Australian Rules footballer Matthew Richardson is 'Richo' to one and all. Oddly, some other names that already end in an -ie sound (like 'Kylie') are often transformed into something else again ('Kyles' in this case).

The ending -zza is also popular, hence the following:

Barry	*Bazza*
Darren	*Dazza*
Gary	*Gazza*
Karen	*Kazza*
Kerry	*Kezza*
Murray	*Muzza*
Sharon	*Shazza*
Terry	*Tezza*

Greetings & goodbyes

G'day is the most famous Australian greeting, so it might surprise you to learn that plain old *Hi* is often much more common, particularly in the cities. Here are some others:

Hey.
Hiya.
How are ya?
How's it going?
How ya goin' mate – orright? (older generation, often male)
How's tricks?

Note that the correct response to any of these questions (as in other English-speaking countries) is almost always 'Good, thanks.'

The handshake is the most widely accepted form of physical contact between strangers or acquaintances when greeting. Hugging and cheek kissing are common between friends and relatives for both greetings and goodbyes, but not between strangers. Of course, this rule is thrown completely out the window when enough alcohol is involved!

Groups of young people may have their own style of handshake, sometimes involving complex knotting of fingers and palms. The high five made its way here from the US and can appear when some form of win has occurred (during a game of footy or a game of pool, for example), but it's not used as a form of greeting or farewell.

Here are a few verbal farewells:

Catch you (later).
Ciao.
Cop you later.
Hooroo! (old-fashioned)
See ya (later).

Talking about the weather

Conversations about the weather in Australia are rarely limited to talk of sunshine or rain. Some parts of the country are subject to unique weather patterns and climatic events that have acquired their own terminology. The country's far north, for example, has two distinct seasons: *the Wet* (roughly November to April) and *the Dry* (May to October). The build-up to the wet season, which takes place during October and into November, can be a hellishly uncomfortable time for locals and visitors alike – temperatures rise, the humidity soars and people tend to go a bit nuts. For this reason, this interim period is also called the *troppo season* or *mango madness* (mangoes are harvested around Darwin and Katherine at this time).

The Tiwi Islands, off the coast of the Northern Territory, have personalised the afternoon thunderstorm that lashes them almost daily during the build-up to the Wet – they call it *Hector*. The type of violent thunderstorm that occurs in the Top End at the end of the Wet is called a *knock 'em down storm*, because it flattens the spear grass that has grown high during the rainy season. In Tasmania, significant rainfall can occur year-round, particularly in the west of the island, which may explain why the locals sometimes refer to rain optimistically as *liquid sunshine*.

The *Fremantle doctor* is a West Australian phenomenon – an afternoon sea breeze that cools both Perth and the West Australian town it's named after. Other West Australian towns have their own versions of this breeze, hence you might hear references to the *Esperance doctor* or the *Albany doctor*, which reaches inland all the way to Kalgoorlie.

Far north Queensland experiences something less pleasant: *the big Bedourie*, which is a large dust storm.

Etiquette

Australians are known for their easygoing nature and friendliness, and have few hard and fast rules about social behaviour. *No worries* is a popular Australian response akin to 'no problems', 'that's OK' or 'sure thing'. There is one exception, however: If you have negative opinions about local places, try to be low-key about it. Though outwardly imperturbable, some Australians will be offended – the older generation in particular can be prone to *cultural cringe* (feeling that one's culture is inferior to that of other countries). Positive opinions, of course, can be easily expressed with true-blue words like *beaut*, *bewdy*, *bonzer* or *ripper*.

For details of the etiquette when it comes to that great Aussie tradition, the pub shout, see page 72.

Among themselves, Australians can make comments that sound to the untrained ear like abuse, but in reality are often mild, good-humoured digs. Australians have a well-stocked arsenal of useful, socially acceptable insults that can be flung at someone else as long as the basic intention is amiable;

accompanying them with a reassuring smile doesn't hurt either. Here are a few, all of which basically mean 'idiot':

bloody drongo   a *drongo* was a horse that came second in all its races

boofhead   possibly derived from the 16th-century word for a fool, 'buffle', which was a borrowed French term of abuse (in French it means 'buffalo')

dumbcluck   referring to the proverbial idiocy of chickens

(you great) galah   a *galah* is a type of bird that has a reputation in Australia for being noisy, gregarious and stupid

nincompoop   someone has suggested that this is a mispronounced version of the Latin phrase 'non compos mentis' meaning 'without control over your own mind', but no one really knows for sure

When a relatively polite, friendly argument takes a serious turn and the participants end up having *a bit of a barney* (an old-fashioned phrase meaning an argument), you may hear one or more of the following terms used to describe it:

argument   bust-up; (wing-)ding; set-to

fight   argy-bargy; barney; blue; box-on; bust-up; donnybrook; dust-up; free-for-all; go-in; punch-up; rough-house; run-in; set-to; yike

The people involved might be described as:

angry   aggro; fit to be tied; foaming at the mouth; hot under the collar; ropeable

crazy   a basketcase; has a few kangaroos loose in the top paddock; lame-brained; the lift doesn't go to the top floor; not the full quid; silly as a two-bob watch; troppo; a wacker

cross with someone dark on someone; dirty on someone; miffed; narked on someone; narky; shirty; snakey; sore

in a bad mood browned off; cheesed off; fed up to the back teeth; has the shits; pissed off; snitchy; uptight; ticked off

Or they might be called names like:

coward a damp squib; dingo; a gutless wonder; nervous Nellie; piker; scaredy-cat; sook; yellow-belly; wimp; wuss

idiot alf; dickhead; goose; imbo (short for 'imbecile'); mug alec; nong; wombat

BRICKIE'S CLEAVAGE

A *brickie's cleavage* is the flash of buttock cleft exposed by low-slung trousers or shorts. This cheeky fashion statement was once confined to labourers who couldn't bear to part with worn-out workwear, but the infatuation with hipsters and homeboy jeans among young Australians has turned city streets into *brickie's cleavage* catwalks.

Here are a few more ear-catching body-part terms you may encounter:

beak	nose
block	head
breadbasket	stomach
bum	buttocks
hunghole	mouth
cakehole	mouth
clodhoppers	feet
crockery	teeth
dial	face
face fungus	facial hair
Gregory Peck	neck
honker	nose
ivories	teeth
laughing gear	mouth
loaf	head
lugs	ears
noggin	head or brains
plates of meat	feet
scone	head

During the fight, some of the following things might happen:

to abuse bore it up someone; get stuck into someone; give someone a blast; give someone heaps; tip the bucket on someone

to be in trouble be in more strife than Ned Kelly; up shit creek

to fight bash up; come to blows; go the knuckle; mix it with someone; stack on a turn

to get scared chicken out; go to water; pack death; pack shit; pike out; take a willy

to lose your temper blow a fuse; blow your stack/top; chuck a mental; chuck a wobbly; crack the shits; cut up rough; do your block/nana; flip your lid; get off your bike; go bonkers; go nuts; go off your brain; go through the roof; lose your cool; spit chips; spit the dummy

to tease chiack; razz someone; rib someone; send someone up; stir; take the mickey out of someone

And of course one of the participants might be told to:

Get lost! Bite ya bum!; Get a big black dog up ya!; Get a rat up ya!; Get knotted!; Get stuffed!; Rack off (hairy legs)!

BASTARD: HANDLE WITH CARE

In Australia, the word *bastard* has an extremely varied job description and it rarely (if ever) refers to illegitimacy. Sometimes it's used in an affectionate way – 'G'day, you old bastard!' – or compassionately – 'Poor bastard lost his job.' But it's just as likely to form part of a string of abusive terms during a fiery exchange, or to be used to describe something annoying ('I can't fix this bastard of a thing!') or someone vile – 'He's a mean bastard.' To confuse you even more, it's also sometimes used to describe *any*one, as in 'Should that bastard be fishing there?' It's best to avoid this (bastard of a) term altogether to avoid putting your foot in it, or at least to tread carefully when using it.

Tourist campaigns over the years have sold Australia as a land of fit, fun-loving (read 'boozy'), laconic, relatively carefree and above all resilient people, perpetually at play, competitive to the last and never short of a tall story or a knowing wink. As with all stereotypes, there's some truth in this. But the collective Australian identity is forged from much more than beer, sport and irony.

Country versus city

The basic division, physically and culturally, for many Australians is between the country (the bush) and the city. Although most Australians live in the cities – which are all, with the exception of Canberra, on the coast – they tend to romanticise the bush and see it as iconically Australian – its flora and fauna, its vast deserts, mountain ranges, rivers and plains.

THE COUNTRY

A number of terms have been created to express the vastness and mythical quality of the landscapes in the country's interior. The best-known example is *the Outback*, a catch-all name for the remote Australian interior. Here are some others:

back of Bourke an unspecified area which is beyond Bourke, a remote town in northwestern New South Wales, on the fringe of the outback. Shorthand for any remote area. *Bullamakanka* and *Woop-Woop* (see page 38) are probably *back of Bourke*.

beyond the black stump   there are a million pubs and motels in New South Wales which claim to have the authentic black stump that explorers went beyond. The phrase most likely came from the practice of giving directions in remote areas based on landmarks like strange-shaped rocks, hills and, of course, the ubiquitous blackened stump.

Bullamakanka   an imaginary remote town which has a pseudo-Aboriginal name and is totally *hicksville*; also called *Woop-Woop* or *Bandywallop*

the Never-Never   this term refers to areas of Queensland and the Northern Territory. There's a theory that the word is an anglicisation of an Aboriginal name for these regions, *Nivah Nivah.* Whatever the truth, the English version conjures up the ultimate state of being lost and forgotten. Jeannie Gunn used this term in the title of her classic 1908 novel about Top End life, *We of the Never-Never*.

A TOWN LIKE ALICE

The Alice is what locals call the town of Alice Springs in the Northern Territory, which lies roughly in the centre of Australia. Alice Springs was named after Alice Todd, wife of the man responsible for the construction of the Overland Telegraph Line completed in 1872, which connected Darwin to Adelaide.

Many Australian country people live on farms or **properties** – in the more remote areas, often on huge **stations** (roughly equivalent to 'ranches' in America), which can be bigger than whole European countries. There are a number of distinctively Australian figures populating the farming stratosphere, including:

cocky farmers   small landholders, so called because they are said to resemble the cockatoo who scratches in the dirt to find food. They come in various flavours: *cane cockies* (sugarcane farmers), *cow cockies* (dairy farmers) and *wheat cockies* (wheat farmers).

grazlers station-owners who run sheep or cattle. The ***grazier*** is likely to be part of the ***bunyip aristocracy*** or ***squattocracy***, the crème de la crème of country society.

jackeroo/jillaroo a ***jackeroo*** or ***jillaroo*** is a young man or woman who works at a station doing various jobs to gain experience

rouseabout a stationhand who's expected to do all the odd jobs. In the shearing shed it's the ***rouseabout*** who rushes up with tar for a cut sheep and takes the fleeces to the sorting table.

Other country folk include the following:

boundary rider the ***boundary rider*** patrols and maintains the fences encircling the vast acreage of an outback station, as well as the incredibly long fences erected by state governments for various reasons (to keep rabbits from crossing into Western Australia or to keep dingoes out of settled New South Wales) Such riders often don't see another human being for months on end, so naturally there's a tradition that they are loners who are happy to be by themselves in the bush.

bushie a ***bushman*** or ***bushie*** is someone who lives capably in the bush. The legend of the bushman is that he's totally at home in the bush and knows all its ways – never gets lost and can always find food and water – and he's usually on good terms with the local Aboriginal people, from whom he's learned a thing or two.

swagman the ***swagman*** or ***swaggie*** is a tramp. He carries his swag ***on the wallaby track*** (shortened to 'on the wallaby') and is often a good bushman too. A ***sundowner*** is a type of swaggie who times his arrival at a station at about sunset – too late to be asked to do any work in return for his tea, sugar and flour.

CLICK GO THE SHEARS

Shearers, the men and women who shear sheep, have their own jargon – masses of it. The champion shearer in each shearing shed, for instance, is called the *gun shearer* or *ringer*. Some other examples are provided by an old song which celebrates this sweaty job, 'Click Go the Shears Boys':

> *The ringer looks around and is beaten by a blow,*
> *And curses the old swaggie with the bare-bellied yeo.*

The *ringer* in this instance is beaten by one blow – that is, one stroke of the shears. And what's worse, he is beaten by an old *swaggie*, a nobody in the shearer's world. The swaggie won by shearing a *bare-bellied yeo* – a ewe that has defective wool growth that makes the wool come off easily.

The places where country folk live and work are often not officially named districts, so in typically practical Australian fashion some areas are identified by the vegetation they contain, as in the following:

the brigalow   this is a kind of acacia or wattle – not an unpleasant tree but one that's difficult to clear for farming because of its habit of suckering. Cattle tend to get lost in it too, and only eat the foliage when they're almost starving. It can also cause *brigalow itch*, a form of dermatitis.

the mallee   *the mallee* can refer to a number of semi-arid areas in New South Wales, South Australia and Western Australia, but is particularly applied to a region in Victoria where *mallee* gums grow. The *mallee* is a species of eucalypt that appears to have no trunk at all (the branches rise straight from the ground), but which does have an enormous and tough root system, a fact that has broken the hearts of many farmers who have tried to dig it out. Mallee root makes good firewood, though, as it's hard and slow-burning.

the saltbush saltbush only grows in salty, semi-desert regions of central Australia where pretty much nothing else will. Despite the obvious drawbacks of its taste, sheep will eat it.

the scrub land covered by shrubby bushes, often dense to the point of being impenetrable and indicating poor soil. To be 'out in the scrub' or 'the scrubs' is to be somewhere unpleasantly remote.

the spinifex this spiny, tussocky grass is mostly found in arid zones of Australia

THE CITY

The city is sometimes referred to by country people as the **big smoke** and its inhabitants as **city slickers**. The general areas where city folk live are rather easier to identify than their equivalents in the sprawling countryside. (However, an increasing number of Australians are leaving the cities to live in small, slow-paced towns by the sea, a phenomenon which is known as a **sea change**.)

the CBD the Central Business District – traditionally anywhere within walking distance of the main post office (called the General Post Office or **GPO**)

the city this is an important and confusing term in Australian English and has various meanings: it can refer, for example, to either the whole of Melbourne or just the Central Business District. A city can also be a large region – you can be driving through the middle of nowhere and find a sign which states that you're now in the City of Bullamakanka. There's a basic distinction between a city, which is very big, and a town, which can be big or small but which is considered less important than a city.

the inner city/suburbs this is the ring of suburbs reaching from just beyond the CBD out to about 7km from the GPO. In Sydney, however, the concept of the inner suburb is more complicated – most people, for example, don't consider North Sydney to be an inner suburb.

the suburbs beyond the inner suburbs are the suburbs proper, which the inner-city coterie may label ***hicksville***. The ***burbs*** have long been the stuff of many middle-class dreams, but are often dismissed by inner-city dwellers as conservative and tediously homogeneous. People who live in the outer suburbs are (stereotypically) considered uncool, ***bevans***, ***bogans***, ***westies***, etc – the antithesis of the inner-city crowd.

GOING TO TOWN

Sometimes you'll hear people say they're 'going to town' for the day, by which they mean they're going to the city centre. They could live ten minutes away but they will still say this.

THE GOOD, THE BAD (& THE UGLY)

Whether they live in the bush, on the beach, in the inner city or in the burbs, Australians generally like to think of themselves as honest, hard-working souls. Perhaps for this reason, Australian English provides terms to make unambiguous distinctions between good and bad people and their actions.

'Good' people can be described in the following ways:

fair dinkum honest, genuine. This expression, which also means 'the truth', comes from the Lancashire dialect in the UK and refers to the basic notion that a fair day's work (or ***dinkum***) demands a fair day's pay. Other terms with a similar meaning include ***the drum***, ***the full two bob***, ***the good guts***, ***the good oil***, ***the griff***, ***the real thing***, ***the straight wire*** and ***true dinks***.

good sport even someone who has never played sport can be described as a ***good sport*** – it means they are good-natured and uncomplaining, accept teasing cheerfully, and are willing to give something or someone a go

plays it straight is fair. Alternatively, ***plays fair*** or ***plays with a straight bat***.

tall poppy a high-achiever. The **tall poppy** is invariably at risk of being cut down by a **knocker** (critic).

upfront honest and/or blunt. Alternatively, **above board, dinky-di, lays it on the line, ridgy-didge** or **straight up and down**.

'Bad' people, or **mongrels** in old-fashioned parlance, take just as many forms. One of the most prominent types is the **bullshit artist** who lies in order to lure you into his latest **lurk** or **rort**. (People are sometimes also labelled bullshit artists when it's thought they're exaggerating or bending the truth.) To **rort the system** is to twist the rules or procedures of an organisation in a manner which is either illegal or bordering on it, for one's own advantage. This used to be popularly thought a political specialty but has spread. **Rorts** are also known as **scams** or **shonks**. Dubious schemes and plans often sound a bit **suss** (suspect), but sometimes you have to **suss them out** (investigate them) in order to realise this. Other descriptions of 'bad' people include the following:

bludger person who lives off other people, either financially or emotionally. A **bludger** can be said to **put the bite on**, **put the fangs into** or **put the nips into** someone. A particularly heinous type is the **dole bludger**, who lives on government benefits because it's easier than working.

cadger a less common word for a **bludger**, a bloodsucker or parasite

dobber person who reports things like **scams**, **rorts**, and **bludging**. One of the contradictions of Australian culture is that those who turn 'bad' people in are often disliked, because they're seen to have somehow offended against the spirit of mateship.

yobbos/yobs uncouth, aggressive people with no subtlety to their antisocial behaviour

Home & family

Middle-class family life in Australia used to be manacled to the notion of the quarter-acre block, where mum, dad and their 1.7 kids (the current national average) would set up home and live the Australian Dream. 'Family' is still a buzzword in contemporary Australian life and the quarter-acre block still lures many parents and their broods out to the suburbs, with their reassuring similitude of housing. But increasingly, homes and their immediate environments take many forms. Following is a list of common housing and residential area terms.

apartment   usually refers to an upmarket (often inner-city) flat, although the term is starting to spread to include all kinds of flats. A *studio apartment* is a small one-room flat.

brick-veneer house   a home with a timber frame and brick exterior. This style of house dominates the burbscape.

California bungalow   the California bungalow is another of the basic house styles of the Australian suburb, and was imported from the goldfields of California in the 1850s. It's typically one storey high with a low-pitched roof, a buttress-like stone or pebble chimney, and a front gable overhanging a verandah upheld by massive stone pillars.

dunny   toilet. Also called a *crapper*, *lav*, *loo* and *thunderbox*. Plumbers are occasionally called *dunny divers*.

duplex   this can be a two-storey block of flats or home units, each dwelling occupying one floor, or a house divided in two vertically

façadism   this practice involves retaining the façade of an old building while constructing a new one behind it

Federation-style   characterised by a red-brick exterior, front verandahs with decorative timber railings, terracotta roof tiles and chimney pots. Houses built in this style date back to between 1890 and 1920.

flat   this is the basic term for a living space in an apartment building or divided house

footpath   pedestrian path on the side of a road (called a 'sidewalk' in North America and a 'pavement' in the UK)

granny flat   a small building in the backyard of a house which can be used as a separate dwelling. Quaintly called a *chalet* in Tasmania.

group house   see *share house*

home unit   a small house sharing a block of land with a number of others. The term may be shortened to *unit*.

laneway   narrow street at the rear of a block of houses, usually originally designed to allow access to garbage collection and, in the days before sewerage, nightsoil collectors (when they were often called 'dunny lanes')

nature strip   a (usually grassy) strip by the side of the road, often between the road and the *footpath*. Called a 'verge' in most other English speaking countries.

Queenslander   common in Queensland (and Darwin, before Cyclone Tracy blew them all down in 1974), these timber homes have wide verandahs and are built on stilts to make the most of cool breezes

semi-detached house   one of a pair of houses joined by a common wall

share house   a house shared by a group of (usually young) people. It's particularly common in the inner city.

Home & family

terrace house   a house joined by common walls to the houses on either side. Paddington terrace houses in Sydney are particularly famous for the charm of the iron lace on their balconies and the wealth of their owners. Various suburbs in other cities also have beautifully restored examples. (Terraces were basically workers' housing of the 19th and early 20th century but have become popular among inner-city dwellers.)

villa   a classier kind of modern terrace house, slightly bigger and with better bathrooms and kitchens

weatherboard   a house clad with overlapping timber boards

MOVING HOUSE

An established business in Queensland is the transplanting of *Queenslander* houses from the original block to another, be it in a neighbouring suburb or a faraway town. As if in a supermarket, buyers meander through rows of these charming timber houses propped up on bricks and choose their dream home. For a fee, the house is sliced in two, lifted onto wide trucks, driven – slowly – to the empty block and 'rebuilt'. Voila!

Education

Australian education generally begins with *kindergarten* or *kindy*, also known as *preschool*. This can comprise the first year of primary school, or the first year may be called *prep* (preparatory). Primary school then generally takes schoolchildren from year one (or first grade) to year six (sixth grade). After this comes *secondary school*, more commonly known as *high school*, which usually lasts from year 7 to year 12. In some rural areas there is a state-run institution called an *area school* or *district school* which provides both primary and secondary education. Also, in some states and territories high school finishes at year 10 and is followed by a *matriculation college* or *secondary college* which looks after years 11 and 12.

The celebrations marking secondary school graduations are known as *schoolies*. The traditional hub of these festivities is the Gold Coast in Queensland, where teenagers flock in their thousands to create alcohol-fuelled chaos during *Schoolies' Week* in November. Students who are accepted into tertiary education will move on to *uni* (university).

The rigours of the primary school day in Australia are alleviated somewhat by a mid-morning break known either as *little lunch*, *playlunch* or *recess*. This is when children stampede into the *canteen* or *tuckshop*, a shop at the school which sells food. Tuckshops were once weighted towards snack foods like pies and chips but in response to burgeoning obesity rates over the last decade or so have generally become much more health-conscious. But as much as kids look forward to recess or lunchtime, nothing compares to getting an *early mark* – to be allowed to go home from school early.

One of the more popular schoolyard games is *British bulldog*, usually played by a large group of boys. One boy stands in the middle of the playground and while the others run past him from one end of the playground to the other he tries to tackle (throw his arms around or bring down) one of them. The captured boy then joins his captor in trying to tackle other boys and the process is repeated until everyone has been tackled. The last boy caught stands in the middle when the next game starts. A less rough version of this game is called *red rover*, which involves tagging (touching) rather than tackling and is favoured by girls.

A less pleasurable playground activity is the *emu parade*, where teachers supervise a group of kids in picking up litter around the school. When this is undertaken as a punishment, it's called *scab duty*. Someone who rarely (if ever) is forced to do scab duty is the *conchie*. Short for 'conscientious', this is a disparaging term for those students who always try to do their utmost best at school, often becoming *teacher's pets*. They would never, for instance, think of *wagging* (intentionally missing school).

Work & politics

The Australian workplace has had its fair share of both success and scandal. The 1970s, for instance, did nothing to improve the image of Australia's corporate accountants. It was during this decade that a number of hard-working accountants (aka *number crunchers* or *bean counters*) devised some intricate, though not technically illegal, methods for minimising company tax. These were called *bottom-of-the-harbour* schemes because the records relating to these dubious transactions were often destroyed or, as it were, 'sent to the bottom of Sydney Harbour'. The expression is now used to describe any *shonky* (dubious) business arrangements.

Australia's political realm is also marvellously idiosyncratic. Australian politicians seem to positively pride themselves on inventing colourful terms of abuse for each other. When the ABC (the Australian Broadcasting Corporation) began broadcasting in Asia, it found that *Parliamentary Question Time* was one of the most popular shows; viewers from Singapore to the Philippines apparently got a kick out of the entertaining abuse. *Drongo*, *dingbat*, *great galah*, *idiot*, *ratbag*, *scum*, *sheep* and *silly old bugger* are some of the terms let fly from the parliamentary benches. Former prime minister Paul Keating was an acknowledged master; he once remarked about Prime Minister John Howard, 'We have blown a hole in [him] on so many occasions that what we have is a dead carcass swinging in the breeze, but nobody will cut it down.'

HOUSEHOLD NAMES: POLITICIANS

Bob Hawke
Labor Prime Minister 1983–91. A former union leader famous for his colourful personal life and his assertion immediately after Australia won the 1983 America's Cup (a yacht race) that 'Anyone who sacks a bloke because he doesn't turn up for work today is a bum!'

John Howard
Liberal Prime Minister. He was first elected in 1996 and has presided over the current era of conservative politics ever since, with strong links to the neo-conservatives in the US administration.

Paul Keating
Labor Prime Minister 1991–96. Among other things, famous for putting his hand on the Queen's back and being labelled the 'Lizard of Oz' by British tabloids.

Jeff Kennett
Liberal Premier of Victoria 1992–99. Kennett had a strong love-hate relationship with the electorate due to his agenda of economic development at any cost and an apparent disdain for social services. He even had a verb based on his name, as in 'We've been Jeffed!'

Love

Australians are relatively uninhibited about love and dating. This is not to say they aren't conservative (many are) but younger people in particular are likely to be upfront about their feelings, or at least their desires. Still, not all locals are comfortable with intimacy – stereotypically, the laconic, blokey nature of many Australian men means they tend to restrain, if not bury, their emotions.

You might come across one of the following terms in discussions on love and sex:

crack onto	chat up (someone)
frenchie	condom
in the raw/nud	naked
pash (on)	kiss passionately
quickie	anything done in a hurry; quick sex
randy	lustful – thus not a popular choice for a child's name in Australia
root	have sex with (a fairly coarse term used mainly by men)
spunk	good-looking person of either sex; similarly *spunk-rat*, but it usually refers to men only
starkers	naked

And finally, there are the common verbs *shag* and *bonk* – light-hearted terms for 'having sex'. Casual partners are sometimes referred to as *bonk buddies*. *Bonk* is a surprisingly popular word, considering it sounds like a cartoon sound effect and doesn't really mean or say anything! Amusingly, it's also used to mean 'to bump', as in 'I bonked my head on the cupboard.'

The national anthem

The Australian national anthem is 'Advance Australia Fair', which replaced the former anthem, 'God Save The Queen', in 1984. Adult Australians rarely find themselves needing to sing the anthem, however, and as a result often struggle to remember the words – after an enthusiastic start, it often becomes a musical mumble.

A song that Australians tend to know better – and usually sing with more gusto – is the unofficial national anthem, 'Waltzing Matilda'. The words contain a whole swathe of Australian colloquialisms from the 19th century:

Once a jolly swagman camped by a billabong
Under the shade of a coolibah tree

The *swagman* is a tramp or wanderer who carries a *swag* - his clothes, cooking implements and so on tied up in a blanket or bedroll. The *billabong* is a waterhole in a river that is otherwise usually dry. The *coolibah* tree is a species of eucalypt found in inland Australia, often in areas which get flooded from time to time (hence the location near the billabong).

And he sang as he watched and waited till his billy boiled
You'll come a-waltzing matilda with me

The *billy* is a tin container used for boiling water for tea. No one is sure where the word comes from but it could come from the Scottish word 'bally', meaning bucket. The origin of the expression *waltzing matilda*, meaning being 'on the road' (as a tramp), is also uncertain. It probably dates back to a German influence on the goldfields, as 'Matilda' is the German equivalent of a *swag*: the 'girl' a man sleeps with when he's alone on the road. Also, the expression 'to waltz' was used to describe German apprentices moving from one town to another to learn their trade.

Down came a jumbuck to drink at that billabong
Up jumped the swagman and grabbed him with glee
And he sang as he shoved that jumbuck in his tuckerbag
You'll come a-waltzing matilda with me

The *jumbuck* is a sheep. This is thought to be Aboriginal pidgin for 'jump up', which is presumably what was most immediately noticeable about sheep. The *tuckerbag* is a bag for holding food. (*Tucker* is a British schoolboy word for food which still survives in Australian English.)

Up rode the squatter mounted on his thoroughbred
Down came the troopers – one, two, three
Whose that jolly jumbuck you've got in your tuckerbag
You'll come a-waltzing matilda with me

In this verse, the strong arm of the law, in the form of *troopers* (mounted police officers), arrives to arrest the swagman for stealing the jumbuck. *Squatters* were originally pioneer settlers on land the government had not got around to officially allocating yet. They became wealthy landowners, part of the *squattocracy*, the new aristocracy of pastoral Australia. This squatter rides a thoroughbred horse and seems to be the lawful owner of the jumbuck.

Up jumped the swagman and sprang into the billabong
You'll never catch me alive said he
And his ghost may be heard as you pass by that billabong
You'll come a-waltzing matilda with me

DANGEROUS AUSTRALIANS

Eventually, it seems, conversations between Australians and non-Australians will always turn to the country's dangerous creatures. And we're not talking about young men driving hotted-up Commodores.* We're talking *critters*.

* a Commodore is a make of car produced by General Motors Holden.

>

<

Australia is home to some of the most poisonous creatures in the world. ('How on earth', foreigners have been known to ask 'have you survived here all these years?') There are three main categories. Firstly, the spiders, the most famous of which are:

funnel-webs (Funnel-web Spiders) a big black hairy spider around 6cm across, common in the Sydney area. The male spiders have an unpleasant habit of wandering around on warm summer nights looking for action, particularly after heavy rain. Bites can be fatal.

redbacks (Redback Spiders) a 2cm to 3cm-long black spider with a bright red stripe on the back. Only the females are big enough to bite. They can give you a nasty shock out at the woodpile or in outdoor toilets, but the bites, though painful, are very rarely fatal.

whitetails (White-tailed Spiders) a small grey or reddish-brown spider with a long cylindrical body that has a whitish spot on the tip. Again, their bites are painful and can cause blisters and swelling, but are not dangerous.

Secondly, of course, there are the snakes. All of the following are highly venomous:

blacks (black snakes, genus *Pseudechis*) including the Mulga or 'King Brown' snake and the Red-bellied Black Snake

browns (brown snakes, genus *Pseudonaja*) found throughout mainland Australia

taipans (*Oxyuranus* species) a more aggressive snake from the north and northeast coast

tigers (tiger snakes, *Notechis* species) usually but not always striped, found along the southeast coast of Australia

Although the snakes and spiders sound fearsome and should certainly be treated with respect, you might be surprised to

>

<

learn that there have been no deaths as a result of spider bites for several decades, and there are only a handful of snakebite fatalities each year (most of which could have been prevented by the application of common sense and first aid). In fact, you're actually in a lot more danger from the idiot in the *speccy* (fancy) Commodore, especially if he's had a few *tinnies*.

Prevention is always better than cure where snakes and spiders are concerned – wear solid boots or shoes when bushwalking, look where you put your feet and hands outdoors, and if you come across one, move away slowly and quietly. In the rare case of a bite from a funnel-web or a snake, forget what you've seen in the movies – there are generally a few hours to get treatment, so don't panic! Dial 000 for an ambulance, have a friend bandage the bitten limb firmly and stay very still. *Don't* wash the bite or apply a tourniquet or attempt to cut or suck the poison out.

In the ocean, however, it's another matter. The third category of poisonous critters is the *stingers*, including such nasties as the *blue-ringed octopus* and the *bluebottle*. The most deadly stinger is the *box jellyfish* of northern Australia. Its tentacles are both transparent and very long, making them difficult to see or avoid, and stings are excruciating and require immediate treatment with antivenom. For your own safety, swim only at netted beaches in affected areas during stinger season. The Australian population hasn't survived here for centuries by taking unnecessary risks!

Holidaying

Anyone taking a *hollie* (holiday) in Australia will find that the country's geographical diversity is reflected in the diversity of places to stay. Besides the usual hotels and motels, travellers can stay in a *pub* (public house) or a *B&B* (bed and breakfast, where breakfast is included in the room rate). Those looking for a place to bunk down in the outback will come across the *donga*, a small room containing only a bed which is sometimes stand-alone but more often lies within a row of similar rooms that collectively resemble a large metal shipping container; *donga* is also the name given to the transportable building containing such rooms. Some holiday-makers choose to take their accommodation with them, hooking up a *caravan* (what Americans call a '(house) trailer') to their car.

NATIONAL HOLIDAYS

New Year's Day	1 January
Australia Day	26 January
Easter	Good Friday, Easter Saturday, Sunday and Monday (March/April)
Anzac Day	25 April
Queen's Birthday	2nd Monday in June (not WA) last Monday in September (WA only)
Christmas Day	25 December
Boxing Day	26 December

Driving

Keen drivers can circumnavigate Australia on the road known as Highway 1, and for an encore can cross the continent from north to south on the Stuart Highway, which links Darwin in the Northern Territory with Port Augusta in South Australia. Once you've got those two trips on nice paved roads out of the way, it's time to strap yourself in and go four-wheel-driving. Australia is criss-crossed with rugged, rutted dirt tracks, which usually began their lives as cattle droving trails. Among the most famous are the 1700km Canning Stock Route and the Birdsville Track.

A common sight on Australian roads is the *ute* (utility truck), which has a rectangular rear tray for transporting goods and equipment, not to mention cattle dogs like the blue heeler. This is also the only place in the world other than New Zealand where you'll see the *panel van*, a two-door van that looks like a swollen station wagon. On the highway, prepare to be intimidated by passing *road trains*. These are semitrailer trucks (prime movers) towing up to four trailers – once they've picked up speed on the open road, they're notoriously reluctant to slow down for anything!

Here are some more terms you'll come across when discussing driving:

click	kilometres, as in 'How many clicks to the next town?'
interstate	in or to another Australian state, as in 'Laura's gone interstate'
median strip	the (usually raised) dividing area between opposing traffic lanes
offsider	companion
park	in relation to driving, this means 'parking space', as in 'I'll try and find a park'
petrol	called 'gas(oline)' in North America

Twenty years ago, many Australians would have sat down each night to the traditional, Anglo-derived dinner of 'meat and three veg' followed by stewed fruit (out of a tin) and custard or jelly (out of a packet). Happily, since that time the culinary offerings of Australia's multicultural society have been enthusiastically accepted, and these days, a standard home-cooked dinner is more likely to involve some kind of pasta or stir-fry. Good use is also made by some people of Australian native or 'bush' foods like wattleseeds, witchetty (*witjutl*) grubs, macadamia nuts, kangaroo, crocodile, emu and bush tomatoes.

What it boils down to for the visitor is plenty of interesting eating, not just in the major cities but in many regional towns too. The same goes for Australian liquids, with international-quality coffee blends, boutique breweries and award-winning vineyards all doing their bit to invigorate the palate.

Eating

Mealtimes in Australia almost need a mini-menu themselves:

brekkie breakfast. On workdays, this commonly consists of things like cereal or muesli with milk (and possibly fruit or yogurt) or toast, butter and *Vegemite* (see page 66), accompanied by a simple *cuppa* (tea or coffee).

morning tea generally *bickies* and a *cuppa* with the occasional indulgence in a cake or bun

brunch a leisurely combination of breakfast and lunch, usually a weekend ritual that involves more elaborate cooked breakfast dishes (eggs with various side dishes, pancakes, and so on)

Eating

57

lunch often consists of one of the endless variations on the theme of some kind of bread product with fillings – whether it be a plain old *sanga* or *sarnie* (sandwich), a *roll* (bread roll) or a filled *pide* (Turkish bread, pronounced 'peedeh'), *focaccia* (Italian bread), bagel or *wrap* (flatbread of some kind wrapped around a filling). Australians also love to 'do' lunch at a café or restaurant.

afternoon tea at work, for most Australians this is a repeat of morning tea. For a luxury treat, though, try the five-star hotels in major cities for a Victorian-era style *spread* of tea, cakes and petite sandwiches.

dinner/tea the main meal of the day. 'Tea', the Northern English term, is becoming less common. Sometimes referred to as *din-dins*, mainly by kids.

Other Aussie terms relating to meals include:

chew'n'spew general name for fast food, reflecting a rather jaundiced view perhaps

counter meal/tea a pub meal, though not necessarily eaten at the *counter* (or bar) and usually cheap – though lots of city pubs have gone upmarket. Standard pub meals include chicken parmigiana (a *parma*), fish and chips, steaks, *bangers and mash* (sausages and mashed potatoes), roast dinners and various pasta dishes.

Devonshire tea scones ('biscuits' to North Americans) with jam and cream and a pot of hot tea. In most country towns you'll stumble across at least one cosy tea (sometimes twee) room serving this popular fare.

junk food general term for any kind of food which is high in accessibility but low in nutrients, like pizza, *Macca's* (food from McDonald's), *lollies* and fried food (or *hot'n'greasies*) such as chips or *dimmies* (dim sims, a kind of large meat dumpling). Fried fish and chips are also sometimes called *fish'n'greasies* or *chish and fips*.

munchies snacks like chips, pies, chocolate bars and so on fall into the category of *munchies*. To have an *attack of the munchies* is to suffer sudden severe pangs of hunger, a fate which befalls dope smokers in particular.

nibblies finger food like nuts, chips and hors d'oeuvres, nibbled on at parties or special *do's* (functions)

nosh an old-fashioned word for food, as in 'Do you feel like some nosh?' In times past people have also used the words *chow*, *grub* and *tucker* to mean the same thing.

(a) spread a magnificent offering of food and drink, the proverbial groaning board. A spread offers you the chance of a *blow-out*, *beanfeast* or *pig-out*.

The following terms are useful to know if you're planning to eat out or picnic in Australia:

BYO	*Bring Your Own* (alcoholic) drinks to a restaurant or party
corkage	the fee charged by restaurants for BYO wines
entrée	on a restaurant menu this is a starter, not a main course as in some other countries
esky	portable ice-box

Typical Australian foods

The Aussie meat pie (in rhyming slang, a *dog's eye*) is a hand-held affair found in pie-warmers in *milk bars*, bakeries, highway *servos* (service stations, aka petrol stations) and even some upmarket cafés, and sold by the thousands at sporting events. A day at the *footy* just wouldn't be the same without a pie'n'sauce (ie ketchup). They're notoriously hotter inside than you expect, so be careful you don't inflict second-degree burns on the roof of your mouth! The traditional beef pie has been supplemented over the years with 'gourmet' concoctions featuring ingredients like Thai curry chicken or beef, spinach and pine nuts.

Also, when you're in South Australia, keep your eyes peeled and your tastebuds primed for the state's native *pie floater* – a meat pie sitting in a bowl of thick pea soup. Don't be scared; many people consider these very tasty, especially on a freezing night or after a few hours of drinking. Ask anyone on an Adelaide city street for the whereabouts of a pie-cart – they'll point you in the right direction.

Here's a list of other typical Australian edibles:

barra	barramundi (fish)
battered sav	saveloy in batter, sometimes called a *dagwood dog* or a *dippy dog* (SA)
bickie	sweet biscuit
brown bread	wholemeal bread
bum-nuts	eggs; also called *cackleberries*, *googies* or *googs* (the 'oo' as in 'put') and *henfruits*
caulie	cauliflower
cheese'n'greens	cheese platter
Chiko roll	a deep-fried bigger cousin of the Chinese spring roll
chips	either potato crisps or French fries, though the latter may be thicker than a classic French fry
chook	chicken
coconut ice	sweet confection consisting of pink and white blocks of dried coconut and sugar
a cut lunch	sandwiches
dead horse	tomato sauce (ie ketchup)
dodger	bread
drumstick	chicken leg
flake	fillet of shark, a popular choice in fish and chip shops

golden syrup	sugar cane syrup
hedgehog	a chocolate slice incorporating crushed biscuits (see page 63 for the recipe)
jam	sweet fruit preserve – North Americans call it 'jelly'
jelly	gelatine dessert – 'jello' in North America
marge	margarine
mince	called 'hamburger meat' in North America
minimum chips	the standard serving of chips available in a fish and chip shop
moo juice	milk; also called *cow juice*
muddie	mud crab (Queensland)
muesli	granola
mushies	mushrooms
nana	banana (pronounced 'narna')
pav	pavlova – a traditional Australian meringue dessert (for the recipe see page 62)
pikelets	little pancakes
prawn	any of a number of species of edible marine crustacean, whether big or tiny
rat coffin	minced meat pie
sausage roll	meat wrapped in flaky pastry; you'll find them beside meat pies in pie-warmers
scones	plain, doughy cakes, called 'biscuits' in the USA (see page 64 for a recipe)
silverbeet	also known as (Swiss) chard
snorkers	sausages; also called *bangers*, *mystery bags*, *snags* and *snarlers*
spag bol	spaghetti bolognese; you may hear this dish referred to as *spaghetti blow-your-nose*
spud	potato
strawbs	strawberries
surf'n'turf	a slab of steak topped with seafood, a typical pub dish
sweets	dessert
toastie	toasted sandwich
yum cha	kind of Chinese restaurant meal in which trolleys loaded with single servings of small dishes (such as dumplings) are sent to diners' tables for them to choose from

CLASSIC AUSSIE RECIPES

Damper

500g flour
1½ teaspoons salt
water

Method

Put flour and salt in a bowl.

Add 3 tablespoons of water and mix.

Form the dough into a ball (you may need to add more water) then flatten into a thick round about 6cm across.

Place the dough among the hot coals of an open fire, cover it with coals and bake for about 30 minutes.

You can wrap the damper in tinfoil prior to baking if you have an aversion to the idea of it being covered in ash.

Serve immediately with butter.

If cooking in a home oven, bake at 180°C for 30 minutes.

Another way to cook damper in the bush is to wrap some around the end of a big stick, cook it in the coals and then pull it off and put a spoonful of golden syrup in the hole.

Pavlova

4 egg whites
pinch salt
250g caster sugar
1 teaspoon white vinegar
1 dessertspoon cornflour

Method

Beat egg whites until stiff and forming peaks.

Add salt, then gradually add sugar.

Add vinegar and beat in well.

Fold in sifted cornflour.

Spread the mixture into a circle on a baking tray.

Bake in oven for 30 minutes at 120°C.

>

<

Turn off heat and leave pavlova in oven for 45 minutes.
When cool, fill with whipped cream and decorate with
strawberries, kiwifruit, passionfruit or sliced banana.

Dancer Anna Pavlova, who the pavlova was named after,
wasn't the only woman honoured in Australia with a dessert.
The Australian-born opera singer Dame Nellie Melba was
the inspiration for the Peach Melba. This sweet concoction
of chilled sponge cake soaked in peach syrup and sherry
and topped with ice cream, almonds and raspberry purée
continues to be a hit in home kitchens.

Hedgehog

300g butter
1¼ cups caster sugar
¾ cup cocoa
3 eggs
2 packets of arrowroot or marie biscuits
1 cup walnuts

For the chocolate icing:
300g dark chocolate buttons
65ml vegetable oil

Method
Melt butter, then add cocoa and sugar.
Stir well on gentle heat until sugar is dissolved.
Remove from heat and cool.
Beat eggs one by one into the butter mixture, then add nuts
and coarsely crushed biscuits.
Line a 2cm-deep baking tray with plastic wrap and press the
mixture into it.
Cover with more wrap and refrigerate for about an hour.

Chocolate icing:
Melt the oil and chocolate over a low heat; spread a layer over
the hedgehog. Refrigerate for a further 30 minutes, then slice
into rectangles.

Pumpkin scones

2 cups self-raising flour
½ teaspoon salt
60g butter
½ tablespoon sugar
1 cup cooked pumpkin, mashed

Method

Add butter and sugar to the sifted flour and salt, and rub the ingredients together in your fingers until the mixture looks like breadcrumbs.

Add the pumpkin, stirring lightly until a soft dough forms.

If the dough is too dry and still crumbly, add a little milk, working it in lightly with a fork.

Gently turn the dough onto a floured board, and pat it out to about 2.5cm thick.

Use a scone cutter to cut it into rounds.

Grease or butter a baking tray.

Place the scones side by side on the tray and bake at 220°C for 15 to 20 minutes.

Anzac biscuits

1 cup plain flour
1 cup rolled oats
¾ cup desiccated coconut
¾ cup sugar
125g butter
2 tablespoons golden syrup
½ teaspoon bicarbonate of soda
1 tablespoon boiling water

Method

Mix the sifted flour, oats, coconut and sugar.

Combine butter and syrup, stir over low heat until melted.

Combine the bicarbonate of soda and hot water and add to the melted butter mixture.

>

<

Stir in the dry ingredients and mix well.

Put teaspoon-size balls of the mixture on a lightly greased oven tray; allow room for spreading.

Bake at 150°C for 20 minutes.

Loosen on trays while warm, then allow to cool.

Makes about 35 *bickies*.

Lamingtons

Bake or buy a basic square or rectangular sponge cake.

For the coating:
2 cups icing sugar
1 tablespoon boiling water
1 tablespoon vanilla essence
2 tablespoons cocoa

Method
Add boiling water and vanilla essence to cocoa.
Stir cocoa mixture into icing sugar and mix well.
Cut the cake into blocks and ice all sides with the coating.
Roll in desiccated coconut.
Allow to dry on wire rack.

There are some food items which have become such a part of the Australian way of life that most locals couldn't imagine doing without them:

Aeroplane jelly comes in pretty packets and in a range of flavours such as 'tropical', mango and lilly pilly (a native fruit). Its famous advertising jingle ('I like Aeroplane jelly, Aeroplane jelly for me!') has been around since the 1930s.

Classic Aussie recipes

65

Arnott's arrowroot biscuit a plain sweet biscuit which is the starting point for a number of desserts or confections

Cherry Ripe Australia's oldest brand of chocolate bar, consisting of cherries and coconut coated in dark chocolate

Coon cheese a kind of basic processed cheddar or 'tasty' cheese; nothing to do with the American 'coon'

Iced Vo-Vo a sweet biscuit topped with fondant, jam and coconut

Sao biscuit a large flaky cracker, traditionally eaten either smothered in butter and ***Vegemite*** or topped with cheese

Tim Tam one of Australia's favourite biscuits, the Tim Tam has a layer of chocolate cream between two chocolate biscuits, with a chocolate coating. The infamous 'Tim Tam Slam' involves biting off diagonally opposite corners of the biscuit, sucking hot tea or coffee through them like a straw, and then cramming the whole biscuit into your mouth before it disintegrates. Don't attempt this in polite society!

Vegemite not a chocolate spread but a salty, vitamin-rich yeast extract from the same family as Promite and Marmite. Commonly spread thinly on toast or crackers (or thickly, depending on the salt threshold of the upper palate in question). Its famous TV ad from the 1950s has given rise to the expression 'happy little Vegemites' – contented and well-behaved children like the ones in the ad.

Violet Crumble a chocolate bar consisting of honeycomb covered in chocolate

APPETISING EXPRESSIONS

Here are a few Aussie expressions you might hear relating to hunger and thirst.

Hunger

I wouldn't mind a bite.

How about a quick bite?

I could eat a horse and chase the jockey.

My stomach thinks my throat's cut.

I could eat the crutch out of a low-flying duck.

I've got the munchies.

Thirst (usually for beer)

I've got a thirst you could photograph.

Your tongue's hanging out.

What about a drop, mate?

How about wetting your whistle?

The second drink

That one didn't touch the sides.

Tide's gone out.

How about anotherie?

I could go another one.

Australian childhoods are punctuated by various sweet treats:

chocolate crackles	balls of puffed rice mixed with chocolate and coconut
cordial	sweet, concentrated syrup you mix with water to create a drink
fairy bread	buttered bread sprinkled with *hundreds and thousands*
fairy floss	known as 'candy floss' in other countries
hundreds and thousands	tiny balls of multicoloured sugar used in cake decoration and to make *fairy bread*
icy pole	frozen sweet flavoured water on a stick
little boys	small frankfurts; also called *cheerios*
lollies	confectionery or sweets
lolly water	soft drink (see below)
soft drink	carbonated nonalcoholic drink

Foreign influences

Not so long ago, *billy tea*, *damper*, *pavlova*, *pie floaters* and *Vegemite* were seen as the only Australian contributions to world cuisine. These days, seekers of a *fair dinkum* Aussie dining experience might find themselves joining the Sunday *arvo* throng in Chinatown for yum cha, delighting in an Italian, Greek, Turkish or Thai banquet, or dining out on snap-fresh sashimi and sushi. Australian migrants have endowed the national cuisine with all the above and more – great coffee, every kind of cheese, superb fresh and cured meats, olives and olive oil, fresh Asian *vegies* like bok choy and gai larn and feisty spices.

SOUVLAKI CITY

Melbourne has the largest Greek population in Australia, so you won't have any trouble finding souvlaki, taramasalata, ouzo and Greek newspapers.

Drinks & drinking

Coffee, beer and wine are considered the Australian drinks of choice, with tea running a close fourth.

COFFEE

If it weren't for the great postwar wave of Italian migration, Australians might still be making coffee out of bottled essence or instant powder. Nowadays, no city restaurant or café would survive without its espresso machine and well-trained staff to crank out cups of java. So worshipped has coffee become in the modern Australian lifestyle that rising real estate prices can be tracked merely by counting the number of espresso machines per head in any given city suburb. And God help you if you're out to impress anyone with social pretensions and you don't know your latte from your macchiato. The exception tends to be remote areas, where the choice in (instant) coffee will probably be limited to 'black or white, love?'

Here are some of the more usual brews available:

caffe latte (often just called a 'latte') half espresso, half steamed milk: slightly frothy and usually served in a glass

cappuccino (aka 'capp') one-third espresso with one-third steamed milk and one-third milk froth, usually topped with sprinkled chocolate powder. Don't be alarmed if your **capp** arrives without the **chokkie** though – it just means you're in a café that chooses to serve cappucinos as the Italians do.

double espresso the post-business lunch power jolt: two short blacks in one cup

flat white two-thirds espresso, one-third steamed milk: no froth, hence the word 'flat'. A flat white is usually served in a cup, if only to distinguish it from a **latte**.

long black order this if you've got the caff-crave for a basic black espresso coffee topped with hot water

long macchiato (long mac) a long black with, as the word 'macchiato' translates, just a 'stain' of cold milk

short black small strong espresso

short macchiato (short mac) an espresso with a 'stain' of cold milk

Then there are the variations. Cappuccinos or lattes also come in soy and **skinny** versions, made with soy and low-fat milk respectively. Any coffee can be ordered **decaf**, too – made with decaffeinated coffee beans. (Before you order, visualise the restaurant scene from Steve Martin's film *LA Story*. While we're on the subject, virtually no one in Australia orders anything with a 'twist' of lemon.) And finally, there's the **babyccino** (milk froth in a tiny cup, topped with sprinkled chocolate powder) – café society training-wheels for kids.

BEER

Lager is the dominant style in Australia and is served ice-cold – a bottle of beer is sometimes just called a *coldie*, as in 'Jeez, I could handle a *coldie* right now.' States remain somewhat loyal to their local beers, but the growing dominance of multinational brewers and distributors means that usually you'll also find interstate and international beers on tap. Even so, in a country pub you may find the choice is Brand X or Brand Y, both owned by Foster's or Lion Nathan. Whether it's VB (Victoria Bitter) in Victoria, Swan in Western Australia, XXXX (pronounced 'four ex') in Queensland or West End in South Australia, the irony of the state brews is that they often don't taste all that different when poured into a glass at a chilly temperature.

You'll find more varied flavours among the produce of Tasmania's Cascade Brewery (Australia's oldest), South Australia's Coopers Brewery and New South Wales' James Squire. The output of microbrewers like Little Creatures (in Western Australia) and Mountain Goat (in Victoria) is also highly regarded and worth sampling. Most microbrewers concentrate on ales, stouts and pilseners rather than trying to compete head-on with the giant lager manufacturers.

Over the past decade, Irish and Belgian pub franchises have been springing up in the major cities. Many are characterless mass-market places trading off the reputations of their templates in Dublin and Brussels, but some have a certain transplanted charm. Pints of Harp Lager, Newcastle Brown Ale and – no surprises here – Guinness are available at prices that can shock the natives but are on a par with the British Isles.

While most Australians agree on the worthiness of drinking beer, the different states have different words for talking about it. See the 'Bottle-O' table, below, for a short guide to some of the state-specific terms relating to beer drinking.

AT THE BOTTLE-O

In a pub

beer	lager in Victoria
bobby	6 oz glass in Western Australia
butcher	6 oz glass in South Australia
glass	5 oz glass in Western Australia
grog	general term for beer or spirits
handle	medium-sized beer glass with a handle
middy	10 oz glass in New South Wales and Queensland; 7 oz glass in Western Australia
pot	10 oz glass in Western Australia, Victoria and Queensland
schooner	15 oz glass in New South Wales and Queensland; 9 oz glass in South Australia
ten	10 oz glass of beer in the Northern Territory (you can also order a *fifteen*)

Takeaway

Darwin stubby	reputedly the largest beer bottle in the world at 2.25 litres
dead marine	an empty beer bottle
echo	small beer bottle in South Australia
sixpack	a pack of 6 bottles
slab	a pack of 24 cans or bottles
stubby	small beer bottle
tallie	large beer bottle (pronounced 'tawlie')
tinnie	a tin of beer; also called a *tube*

Drinks & drinking

PUBS

A pub is the best place in which to start sampling the various styles and sizes of Aussie beer. A pub can be anything from a small bush shanty with a bar and verandah to a glossy, groovy, cosmopolitanised city number. If it's close to home and a favoured haunt then it's known as *the local*; other pet names include *the rubbidy* (rhyming slang – *rubbidy dub* means 'pub'), *the pisser* or *the boozer*. Most pubs have a *bottle shop* (*bottle-o* in South Australia) to sell takeaway beer, wine and so on, and it often has a drive-through facility. There are also *bottle shops* which operate independently of pubs.

THE SHOUT

The great Australian *shout* (in rhyming slang, a *wally grout*) is a well-established custom in pubs and bars. Individuals in a group take turns buying everyone a drink – this is called buying a *round of drinks*. It can put a real strain on your wallet, depending on the size of the group and what they're drinking! Remember that it's not obligatory to take part – you can just decline the offer of a shout and buy your own drinks. This may be seen as bad form in certain hard-core bars where reputations are made and lost on the basis of how much someone can drink in relation to everyone else, but generally your non-participation won't bother anyone. The most important thing is not to let someone else shout you a drink if you've got no intention of (or no money for) reciprocating.

WINE

In barely 35 years, Australian wine has become a multibillion dollar industry, and new wineries and vineyards continue to spring up. Australia now ranks in the world's top 10 wine-making countries.

Before the 1970s, table wines weren't popular and sherry and port ruled supreme – these and other fortified wines such as muscats and tokays (sometimes called *stickies*) aren't as fashionable these days, although those produced at Rutherglen in northeastern Victoria can be superb.

At time of writing Australia is awash with grapes, and there are many $10 to $15 bargains to be had, both from traditional outlets and from the increasing number of bottle shops dedicated to *cleanskins* – unbranded wines. As far as varieties go, in Australia shiraz is arguably still king. *Grange* (Penfolds Grange Hermitage) is an acknowledged world leader in the style and commands amazing prices at auction. Pinot noir is another red-hot style, so much so that a word, *pinophile*, has been coined to describe a pinot noir fanatic. However, there are still many loyal lovers of old favourites like *chardy* (chardonnay), *cab sav* (cabernet sauvignon) and the recently fashionable riesling, and the main party season (roughly November to January) still floats on a tide of *bubbles* (sparkling wine, aka *champers*).

Following is a list of Australia's main wine types and the regions that produce the best of each style. Expect to pay $20 plus at a shop or $35 plus in a restaurant for a decent-quality wine (and about 20% more for the heavy reds).

Whites

chardonnay	Clare Valley (SA), Hunter Valley (NSW), Margaret River (WA), Mornington Peninsula (Vic)
pinot gris	Mornington Peninsula (Vic), Yarra Valley (Vic)
riesling	Clare Valley (SA), Eden Valley (SA)

sauvignon blanc	McLaren Vale (SA), Padthaway (SA), Yarra Valley (Vic)
semillon	Hunter Valley (NSW), McLaren Vale (SA), Margaret River (WA)
sparkling white	Adelaide Hills (SA), Tasmania, Yarra Valley (Vic)
verdelho	Hunter Valley (NSW), Margaret River (WA)

Reds

cabernet sauvignon	Coonawarra (SA), Mudgee (NSW), Margaret River (WA), Yarra Valley (Vic)
merlot	Langhorne Creek (SA), Mudgee (NSW)
pinot noir	Mornington Peninsula (Vic), Tasmania, Yarra Valley (Vic)
rosé	Barossa Valley (SA), Yarra Valley (Vic)
shiraz	Hunter Valley (NSW), McLaren Vale (SA), Mudgee (NSW), Padthaway (SA)

Following is some of the shorthand favoured by Australian wine-lovers:

bin a term from the stock-keeping system of the Penfolds group, sometimes seen on labels (ie Bin 707)

cab merlot a blend of cabernet sauvignon and merlot

cask wine typically cheap and cheerful wine packaged in a plastic bladder inside a cardboard box. This Australian invention is sometimes called **chateau cardboard**.

dryland unirrigated vineyards

Grange Hermitage the nation's most famous red, created by late legendary winemaker Max Schubert *plonk*   cheap wine; also called *bombo*, *red ned* and *steam*

Southcorp   the dominant company in the industry, encompassing brands such as Seppelts, Penfolds, Seaview, Kaiser Stuhl and dozens of others

sparkling red   sparkling wine made from red grapes such as shiraz, cabernet sauvignon and merlot – an Australian speciality. Also called *sparkling burgundy*.

sparkling wine   slang terms for this include *bubbles*, *champers*, *fizz*, *le pop*, *shampoo* and *wa-wa juice*

vino   general term for wine

GROGGING ON

The sheer number of terms that have been invented to describe drinkers, drinks and drinking situations gives you an idea of how entrenched alcohol is in Australian culture:

alkie	an alcoholic
amber fluid	general term for beer; also called *slops* or *suds*
bevvie	short for 'beverage'; almost always refers to a beer
booze bus	police van used for random breath testing for alcohol
coldie	cold bottle or can of beer
drink with the flies	to drink alone
duck's dinner	drinking with nothing to eat
frostie	cold bottle or can of beer
grog on	to drink alcohol over quite a long period of time; also to *kick on*
hair of the dog (that bit you)	alcohol drunk to ease a hangover

>

<	
heart-starter	the first alcoholic drink of the morning after a hard night's drinking
on the turps	currently in the habit of drinking vast amounts of alcohol
pig's ear	beer
pub crawl	usually a group activity, involving drinking at a number of pubs in one evening
put on the wobbly boot	to get drunk
sherbet	alcoholic beverage
sit on a beer	to drink a beer slowly
sundowner	a beer drunk in the late afternoon; mainly used in the NT
tinnie	can of beer

Australians love watching sport. In fact, watching sport has become a sport in itself in Australia, and there are various rules to follow: ideally, find a big-screen TV at a mate's place or go to one of the pubs that get sports channels beamed in via satellite; have the fridge well-stocked with alcohol and the coffee table littered with snacks; discuss the sport at every opportunity while watching it, even if you're not that interested in proceedings, etc. An appreciation of all things sporty is drummed into many Australians from an early age. Sportspeople give talks at schools and are held up as healthy role models (they've given up on Shane Warne though), and parents dress children up in the colours of their favourite football team and take them to games as toddlers to indoctrinate them.

The main sports in Australia are *footy* (football) and cricket. The term *footy*, however, refers to different codes of football in different states: mainly to Australian Rules in the southern and western states and Rugby League in New South Wales and Queensland. To add to the confusion, Australian soccer has rebranded itself as 'football' as well, bringing itself in line with the international name of the game.

Australian Rules football

This uniquely Australian sport, invented in 1858, is commonly referred to as *Aussie Rules*, or more imaginatively as *aerial ping-pong*. It's played around the country in local and regional competitions as well as in the national competition, the AFL, or Australian Football League. The season runs from March to September, and the game is played on an oval up to 185 metres from end to end with four posts at each end: two inner, taller ones called 'goal posts', and two smaller, outer ones called 'behind posts'. Teams of 18 (plus up to four interchange players) aim to kick an oval ball cleanly between the goal posts, thereby scoring a goal (six points). If the ball is touched on its way, or touches the post, or goes between a goal post and a behind post, it's worth a **behind** (one point). Scores of 20 goals or more by one or both teams are common. There are four quarters of 20 minutes each plus **time on** – time added due to stoppages.

The winning team is the team with the highest number of points at the end of the game – drawn games are rare. Tackling is fierce, and only tackling above the shoulder or below the knees and pushing in the back are banned. If the ball is kicked, goes through the air for more than 15 metres and is caught, the player who catches it is awarded what's called a **mark** by the **umpire** (referee) and takes a free kick. Throwing the ball is barred, but a handball – holding the ball in one hand and hitting it with a clenched fist – is okay. Visit www.afl.com.au for the full rules and current news on the game.

It's traditional when attending a footy match that you **barrack** for a team as loudly as possible. In some countries **barracking** means 'abusing the opposing team', but in Australia it means to 'cheer on a team'. You'll often hear the following words being yelled out during a game:

Avagoyermug!	'Have a go, you mug!' – traditional rallying call, also used at cricket matches
Carn!	'come on', as in 'Caarn the Saints!'
Chewie on ya boot!	aimed at distracting a footballer on the verge of kicking a goal (**chewie** is chewing gum)

And football commentators and spectators use the following to describe on-field actions:

got coat-hangered	was hit by a straight arm
got dragged	was taken off the field by the coach
had a blinder	played really well
took a speccy	took a spectacular high mark

THE TEAMS
Following are the 16 teams that play in the AFL. Key venues include the MCG (Melbourne Cricket Ground, where the AFL Grand Final is held), SCG (Sydney Cricket Ground), Gabba (Brisbane Cricket Ground), AAMI Stadium (in Adelaide), Subiaco (in Perth) and Telstra Dome (in Melbourne).

Adelaide	the Crows
Brisbane Lions	the Lions
Carlton	the Blues
Collingwood	the Magpies or Pies
Essendon	the Bombers
Fremantle	the Dockers
Geelong	the Cats
Hawthorn	the Hawks
Kangaroos	the Roos
Melbourne	the Demons or Dees
Port Adelaide	Port Power
Richmond	the Tigers
St Kilda	the Saints or Sainters
Sydney	the Swans
West Coast Eagles	the Eagles
Western Bulldogs	the Doggies

YA DROP KICK

There are many ways of describing how the oval-shaped ball is kicked, from recognised kicking actions to descriptions of intent or the consequences of a poor kick: ***checkside*** or ***banana kick***; ***drop kick*** (out of fashion as a kick, but in fashion as a term of verbal abuse); ***drop punt***; ***hospital ball***; ***lean back and go bang***; ***mongrel punt***; ***a rain maker***; ***screwie***; ***set sail for home***; ***stab pass***; and a ***torp***.

THE POSITIONS

full-back line	two back pockets and one full-back
half-back line	two half-back flanks and one centre half-back
centre line	two wingers
half-forward line	two half-forward flanks and one centre half-forward
full-forward line	two forward pockets and one full-forward
centre square	one ruckman, one ruck rover and two rovers

MAJOR EVENTS

The AFL Grand Final takes place on the last Saturday in September and is attended by in excess of 90,000 people and watched on TV by millions.

Another significant AFL event is the televised presentation of the Brownlow Medal, awarded to the player judged best and fairest by the umpires over the whole season. It's actually quite a dull affair, typically watched either by football addicts or by those who take an active interest in the skimpy outfits worn by footballers' wives and girlfriends.

SOME AUSSIE RULES IDENTITIES

Bob Skilton

Star of South Melbourne – now Sydney – during the 50s and 60s and three-time winner of the Brownlow medal.

Chris Judd

West Coast midfielder with a blistering turn of speed. Winner of the 2004 Brownlow Medal in only his third year of AFL football and of the Norm Smith medal (for best afield) in 2005.

Dermott Brereton

'Dermie' – flamboyant, mischievous and skilled Hawthorn half-forward of the 1980s, now a television commentator.

Gary Ablett (Sr)
Known as 'God' by adoring Geelong fans. A magnificent full-forward of the 1980s and 90s, he topped the goal-kickers' table three times and won the Norm Smith Medal in the 1989 Grand Final.

James Hird
Respected former Essendon captain with a reputation for single-handedly turning games around.

Kevin Sheedy
Highly successful coach of Essendon for over 25 years, and former Richmond star. Essendon have won four premierships under him.

Leigh Matthews
Uncompromising Hawthorn star of the 1970s and 80s and now three-time premiership coach of Brisbane.

Michael Voss
Inspirational captain of Brisbane, who led his team to a hat-trick of premierships in 2001, 2002 and 2003.

Nathan Buckley
Talented, ambitious Collingwood captain regarded as one of the great players of the modern era.

Ron Barassi
Former Melbourne and Carlton star best known for his highly successful coaching career.

Tony Lockett
'Plugger', a man-mountain full-forward who broke Gordon Coventry's long-standing goal-kicking record by amassing 1357 goals for St Kilda and Sydney (collectively) before retiring in 2002.

Ted Whitten

'Mr Football', Footscray legend of the 1950s and 60s (Footscray are now known as the Western Bulldogs) who will always be associated with the Victorian State-of-Origin team. He was given a state funeral in 1995.

Rugby league

Traditionally this is the main winter sport in New South Wales and Queensland, although Aussie Rules has made major inroads in the past decade or so, particularly up north due to the success of the Brisbane Lions. 'League' broke away from rugby union in England in the 1890s, many of the rules changed and it rapidly became semi-professional at the top level. It had spread to Australia (and New Zealand) by 1908 but isn't as well known as rugby union worldwide. The ground (with large H-shaped posts at either end), the ball and the general nature of play are similar to (and in many ways simpler than) union, but most visitors to Australasia will find some details unfamiliar (unless they come from the right part of England!).

There are 13 players on a team (plus *reserves*, ie substitute players). They attempt to get the oval ball past their opponents by handpassing it (always backwards) or kicking it (forwards). Placing the ball on the ground behind the goal line scores a try (four points) which can then be 'converted' by a place kick through the H and over the bar (two more points). There are also penalty goals (two points again) and field goals (one point). A tackled player regains his feet and heels the ball backwards to a colleague, so there's no *rucking* (where players roll the ball with their feet when it's on the ground) or *mauling* (wrestling the ball away from others) as in rugby union – after six tackles the other team gets possession. The opposition can also get possession if the ball goes 'out of play' over the sidelines. See www.australianrugbyleague.com.au if you'd like more information.

THE TEAMS

There are 16 teams in the National Rugby League (NRL), all of which are based on the east coast with the exception of teams from Melbourne and Canberra, and a trans-Tasman team from Auckland.

THE POSITIONS

Seven backs (one fullback, four three-quarter backs, one five-eighth, one halfback) and six forwards (two props, one hooker, two locks, one loose forward).

MAJOR EVENTS

The finals are held in September, culminating in the Grand Final which is held in Sydney. As well, each year New South Wales and Queensland teams are selected to meet in the three 'State of Origin' matches: rugby league at its best. In international rugby league there's a World Cup tournament at which 10 teams play (having first won their qualifying matches), as well as an annual Tri-Nations competition between Australia, New Zealand and Great Britain.

SOME RUGBY LEAGUE IDENTITIES

Andrew Johns

The driving force behind the Newcastle Knights, and template for the complete modern player. He stamped his class on the 2005 State of Origin series to ensure a NSW victory.

Allan 'Alfie' Langer

Superb halfback and an icon of Queensland rugby league, who retired in 2002 after a nearly 20-year career in the game.

Darren Lockyer

Brisbane Broncos and Queensland captain, a fullback turned five-eighth who is a brilliant attacking player.

Rugby union

Rugby union is the older code of rugby – in Australia it's often called just 'rugby', in contrast with 'league' – and is better known around the world than rugby league. It was strictly amateur even at the top till the mid-1990s. Until the late 1970s Australia struggled to compete on the international stage, but since then the national team, the Wallabies, have grown to be a dominant force in rugby. They have won the coveted World Cup twice since its inception – the only team to do so.

An international competition called the Super 14 involves regional teams from Australia, New Zealand and South Africa. There's also the Tri Nation Series between these three southern hemisphere giants of the game.

Rugby union is played 15 a side (eight forwards). Tries are worth five points, conversions two, penalty goals and field goals three. 'Set plays' (preplanned *scrums*, *rucks*, *mauls* and *line-outs*) are more important than in league. See the Australian Rugby Union website, www.rugby.com.au, for more details.

SOME RUGBY UNION IDENTITIES

John Eales
One of the greats of Australian rugby, he played for the Wallabies for 10 years up to 2001 and participated in two World Cup victories.

Mark Ella
A brilliant player who was instrumental in the rise of the Wallabies in the early 1980s. Ella stunned the rugby world by retiring in 1984 at the age of just 25.

George Gregan
Long-serving Australian captain and aggressive, nuggety scrum-half.

HOUSEHOLD NAMES: SPORTS STARS

Layne Beachley
Women's world surfing champion for six consecutive years from 1998 to 2003.

Michael 'Mick' Doohan
Multiple world 500cc motorcycle champion, who retired in 1999.

Dawn Fraser
Former champion Olympic swimmer and now tireless community worker. She was awarded an Order of Australia in 1998.

Cathy Freeman
An outstandingly successful Aboriginal middle-distance runner who won gold in the 400 metres at the 2000 Olympic Games. She retired in 2003.

Lleyton Hewitt
Hewitt was ranked the world number one tennis player in 2001 and 2002, and is famous for aggressive self-motivation techniques that include a tendency to yell 'Come on!' into his fingertips during matches.

Lauren Jackson
Basketballer who was drafted by the Seattle Storm in 2001 and voted Most Valuable Player in the prestigious American WNBA (Women's National Basketball Association) in 2003.

Greg Norman
World-class golfer, winner of several majors and known as the 'Great White Shark'.

Ian Thorpe
Great long-distance Olympic swimmer and world record holder, sometimes known as the 'Thorpedo'.

Football (soccer)

The world game has traditionally been the poor relation of other football codes in Australia, and has historically lacked popular support, being thought of as an immigrant's sport. The main competition, the A-League, is national and is played in the summer. The main catalyst for the sport's growth in the 1990s was the fairly consistent and sometimes excellent form of the national team, the Socceroos, and a growing interest in watching the World Cup. In 2005 the sport was officially rebranded as 'football' in Australia, instead of 'soccer', in an effort to bring it into line with its international peers.

REVHEADS UNITED

When the Australian leg of motor racing's Formula One Grand Prix series was poached from Adelaide in 1994, an area of the inner Melbourne suburb of Albert Park was altered to host the event, much to the fury of local residents. Every March the lakeside park roars to the sound of engines and racing enthusiasts (known as *revheads* or *petrolheads*).

Cricket

Despite various competing attractions, the quintessential Aussie summer sport is still cricket, transplanted from England in colonial times. For those who aren't acquainted with the game, the best way to begin to understand it is to go to a match with someone who's familiar with the rules and can shed light on the arcane proceedings.

One-dayers – single-day matches in which each side bats once – are increasingly popular, but are regarded by traditionalists as travesties of 'real' Test cricket, which can last four days at state level and five at international level. The *bowler* (pitcher) must 'bowl' the ball at the batsman with a straight arm and not throw it, although fielders can throw it. Six balls (an *over*) are bowled at one of the two sets of stumps, which is defended by one of the two batsmen who are 'in' at any given time. After an over, the whole fielding side (but not the batsmen) change ends and a different bowler bowls the next over at the other set of stumps. This goes on until the innings ends, which usually takes hours (50 to 150 overs).

There are a number of ways the bowler can get a batsman out (which is called *taking a wicket*), the two simplest being to hit the stumps or to induce the batsman to hit the ball up in the air and be caught out. The wicket-keeper behind the stumps is the prime catcher. Batsmen remain at bat until dismissed; when 10 of the 11 in the team are out, the team's *innings* is over (ie the other team takes its turn batting).

Each time the batsmen are able to run past each other and change ends a run is scored. If the ball crosses the boundary the batsman gets four runs, and six runs if it goes over the boundary without touching the ground. Surprising as this may seem to baseball fans, the batsmen aren't required to hit all the balls bowled at them, though missing or ignoring an accurate ball may lead to dismissal by being 'bowled' (having the ball hitting the stumps)! If the batsman *does* hit the ball, he doesn't have to run (another surprise!) – this is a decision to be made by the two batsmen and depends on the risk of being run out (where the stumps are hit by the ball while a batsman is still out of his *crease*, the painted line at his end of the cricket pitch) and the state of the game. A great score by one batsman would be 100 or more and a top bowler can hope to get five or more of the possible 10 *wickets* (dismissals) in an innings.

The teams for the main domestic competitions represent the Australian states. The national team regularly plays Test and one-day matches against nine other nations: New Zealand, South Africa, Zimbabwe, Pakistan, India, Bangladesh, Sri Lanka, the West Indies and England. The Australian team has a track record as one of the best in the world.

THE RIVALRY BEGINS

The first international cricket tour of England was in May 1868, by a team of Aboriginal cricketers whose 17 members had already played at the Melbourne Cricket Ground and toured Sydney. In six months they played 47 matches against the English – victorious in 14, defeated in 14 and drawing 19. On return to Australia, the two most outstanding players – Johnny Mullagh and Jimmy Cuzens – were signed up by the Melbourne Cricket Club.

WOMEN'S CRICKET

Women's cricket in Australia boasts an illustrious history on a par with the Australian men's cricket teams. The first women's team was established in 1874 with a local match in Bendigo, Victoria. The first Test match was played in Brisbane in December 1934, between teams from Australia and England. The women's team first toured England in 1937, New Zealand in 1948–49 and India in 1975.

The Australian women's team competes in an international competition involving 10 other teams and in 2005 was ranked number one in both one-day and Test cricket. It has won four Cricket World Cups (a competition that began in 1973, two years before the introduction of the men's Cricket World Cup).

There are around 26,500 female cricketers playing at school and club levels throughout Australia.

SOME CRICKET IDENTITIES

Adam 'Gilly' Gilchrist

Wicket-keeper and brilliant attacking batsman who revolutionised the one-day game with his quick, destructive batting at the top of the order.

Dennis Lillee

One of the game's finest fast bowlers, adored by Australian crowds in the 1970s and early 80s.

Karen Rolton

Fast-scoring top-order batter and left-arm pace bowler, the mainstay of Australia's world champion women's team and the best all-rounder the women's game has seen.

Sir Don Bradman

The greatest batsman ever, garnering an amazing Test average of 99.94 (an average of almost 40 runs per match higher than the next three best batsmen) in a career lasting from 1928 to 1948.

Shane Warne

The greatest leg spin bowler of all time and the game's best wicket-taker at Test level, with 583 and counting. His greatness on the field has been overshadowed by numerous off-field controversies, including allegations of marital infidelities.

SLIP, SLOP, SLAP

It doesn't qualify as a sport, but *sunbaking* (sunbathing) has certainly been a national pastime, not just on beaches but also during long cricket matches and other sporting events. Unfortunately, the habit of exposing skin to the blazing Australian sun has given the country one of the world's highest rates of skin cancer. The first and most famous skin cancer awareness campaign, in 1981, urged people to 'Slip, slop, slap – slip on a shirt, slop on suncream and slap on a hat.' It and later campaigns have met with varying degrees of success.

Surf lifesaving & surfing

Surf lifesaving in Australia started at Manly Beach in Sydney in 1902, when a daring William Gocher broke the law by bathing in daylight. In the years that followed, 'leisure' swimming at beaches became a popular activity and drownings a common occurence. In response to these dangers of the sea, the New South Wales Surf Bathing Association was formed in 1907, and later became a national body. Its members, who now number over 100,000 in some 280 clubs around the country, have performed hundreds of thousands of rescues, and the national championships attract large crowds. The probability of drowning in Australia is dramatically reduced when swimming between the warning red and yellow flags set up by the Surf Lifesaving Association.

Surfing was first demonstrated to intrigued Australians in 1915, when a Hawaiian called Duke Kahanamoku rode his hand-carved surfboard at Freshwater, on Sydney's north shore. Today, local surf beaches are clogged with surfers of all ages waiting for the next swell. Australia boasts several world champions and international surfing events, including the Rip Curl Pro contest (see the box on page 92) at Bells Beach in Victoria.

Basketball

Although many people think of basketball as a quintessentially American sport, it has a very respectable participation rate in Australia – around 220,000 men, women and children are registered as playing in some kind of basketball team each year and it's estimated that around 600,000 play in some capacity. Basketball's history in Australia is also surprisingly long. The first game in the country was played in 1905 at the Melbourne YMCA and the sport's governing body, Basketball Australia (then called the Australian Basketball Federation), was founded in 1939. It became a member of FIBA, the International Basketball Federation, as early as 1949.

Today, the main professional competition is the National Basketball League or NBL, in which 12 region-based teams play a season that runs from October to April. The parallel women's league, the WNBL, has eight teams – and rather less television coverage. The second-tier competition, which also forms a recruiting pool for the NBL and WNBL, is organised by the Australian Basketball Association and consists of about 120 small local teams.

While the men's national team, the Boomers, isn't quite in the league of teams from nations such as the US or Lithuania (and has never won an Olympic medal), the Opals, the women's team, has an impressive record. The Opals have won medals at every Olympics they've attended, including silver at Sydney in 2000 and at Athens in 2004.

SOME BASKETBALL IDENTITIES

Andrew Bogut

A seven-foot Melbourne boy and the son of Croatian immigrants, Bogut is a rising star in the American NBA after being picked up by the Milwaukee Bucks in the 2005 draft. He was the number one draft pick of that year – meaning Milwaukee, who won the lottery for the right to first choice, thought he was the best young player available in the draft.

Andrew Gaze

Arguably Australia's best male basketballer, with brilliant shooting skills and a record seven Most Valuable Player awards. Gaze retired in 2005 after a career that included two NBL championships and five Olympic Games.

Lauren Jackson

One of the world's best female basketballers. Jackson won three consecutive premierships for the Canberra Capitals in the Australian WNBL, played for the Opals in the 2000 and 2004 Olympic Games (at both of which the team won silver), and plays for the Seattle Storm in the American WNBA. She won Most Valuable Player of the WNBA in 2003 and led the Storm to the 2004 WNBA Championship.

Luc Longley

Two-time Olympian and the first Australian player to be drafted to the American NBA. Most of his career took place in the US, where he won three NBA championships with the Chicago Bulls in the 1990s.

GREAT RACES

Birdsville Races
These races may not get the media coverage of the Melbourne Cup (see page 136), but as Australia's premier outback horse race, the Birdsville Races on the first weekend in September are a hugely popular event. And the beer starts flowing early …

Rip Curl Pro
Each Easter weekend, Bells Beach (southwest of Melbourne) attracts top surfers and wannabes to the world's longest-running professional surfing competition.

Sydney to Hobart Yacht Race
For the start of this race on Boxing Day, Sydney Harbour is crammed with hundreds of seacraft from cruisers to dinghies as the competing yachts sail off toward Tasmania. There's a huge street party in Hobart to celebrate the end of this long event.

Netball

Netball was created by an American basketball coach based in England who set himself a challenge to improve the skills of his charges. This new game was introduced to several schools in England, where it became a popular sport, particularly with women, and quickly spread to Australia. In recent years, Australian teams have been prominent in worldwide netball competitions. Although initially netball was characterised as a female sport, growing interest by men led to the formation of men's and 'mixed' netball teams.

A netball court is approximately the size of a tennis court with a shooting semicircle and goal post at each end. The goal post has no backboard, just a simple hoop for shooting goals – It doesn't, as the name 'netball' may suggest, resemble the netted basket of basketball.

Each team has seven players:

- goal shooter
- goal keeper
- goal attack
- goal defence
- wing attack
- wing defence
- centre

Each position is restricted to a specific area on the court; only the goal shooters are allowed to shoot goals and only from inside the semi-circle. A player can only move two steps once they have possession of the ball and are permitted to hold the ball for only three seconds.

The rules of indoor netball differ slightly to the sport's outdoor version – these differences mainly involve court size, game duration and the presence of nets around the court.

There are 654 netball associations in Australia, and it's estimated that 1.2 million Australians play netball, counting those involved in school, mixed, men's and indoor netball competitions. Netball was trialled at the 1994 Commonwealth Games and introduced as an official sport at the 1998 Games, where the Australian women's team won the gold medal. The team won the world championships the following year and were runners up to New Zealand in 2003.

WHAT'S IN A NAME?

As if sport statistics weren't enough to remember, sport fans in Australia also need to keep up with the changing names of the sports grounds. Since the late 1990s, Australian sporting facility managers have followed the lead of those overseas and turned once stable names into a rotating business who's who. A ground called Kardinia Park (in Geelong near Melbourne), for example, became first Shell Stadium and then Skilled Stadium. Confusingly, there are now two stadiums sponsored by the same company – Telstra Stadium in Sydney and Telstra Dome in Melbourne. Perhaps the facility managers simply enjoy testing commentators' memories?

Australians are masters at entertaining themselves (and each other), be it by spending their hard-earned cash in shopping malls or boutiques, catching a movie or a play, staring blankly at a television screen, or succumbing to the spirit of the occasion at a live gig, party or festival.

Aussies will seize on just about any excuse for a celebration, so it'll be an extremely rare week (or even day) that there's not a festival of some kind being staged somewhere.

Live music & clubs

Inner-city pubs and many of their small-town equivalents used to be bastions of live music, where you could go to see Australian bands (usually rock, blues and acoustic/folk outfits) up to several times a week. But in many inner-city areas at least, the stage has been stowed away to make room for poker machines. That said, there are still plenty of hotel venues (particularly in capital cities like Melbourne and Sydney) that frequently host local and international acts. A lot of night – and day – life centres on the pub (especially in country towns). Families come early for a *counter meal*, others linger with mates and a beer or six, play darts or shoot pool (many pubs have pool teams and regular tournaments), or tune into some live rock'n'roll.

There are also plenty of clubs in country and suburban areas around which the social life of the community revolves. Such watering holes include sporting clubs, most notably football clubs which have associated football teams and offer extensive drinking and gambling facilities, and RSL (Returned & Services League) clubs, the local chapter of which is sometimes called the *Rozzer*. The other kind of club is a nightclub to which a *punter* (the average person/customer) will go, after kickstarting the night in a bar or café – to drink and dance, often until the sun comes up. Australian liquor licensing laws in some areas mean that if you really wanted to you could start out on Friday, get home on Monday, and not stop dancing, drinking or socialising in-between – except maybe for some power naps. Take your pick between multi-level dance clubs (maybe hip-hop up the top, hardcore trance in the middle, lurved-up house down below) or laid-back grooves at fashionable lounges.

Movies, TV & theatre

Australians are ranked among the biggest cinema-goers in the world, with ticket sales increasing every year, and there's no shortage of cinemas and films (*flicks*) for your viewing pleasure. Small 'art-house' cinemas show foreign-language and avant-garde films, while large companies like Hoyts and Village compete to show the blockbusters and big names. During the summer months, *moonlight cinemas* are popular – you can catch a film at night under the stars as you lounge on a picnic blanket or in a deck chair. It's worth noting that most cinemas offer half-price sessions, generally either on a Monday or Tuesday.

Australian commercial television is largely dominated by American and British imports and re-runs and soap operas like *Neighbours*. The pop culture monotony is alleviated, however, by the government-sponsored ABC channel and its multicultural offshoot, SBS. All of the country's major cities have thriving arts scenes and even the smallest country towns will have a repertory theatre group.

HOUSEHOLD NAMES: ENTERTAINERS

Russell Crowe
Technically a Kiwi (New Zealander), but claimed by Australians as their own. An Oscar-winning actor, though also famed for his bad temper and responsible for the underwhelming band 30 Odd Foot of Grunts.

Paul Hogan
Comic actor, previously a Sydney Harbour Bridge worker and then TV comedian. Known for the *Crocodile Dundee* movies and for his ads enticing Americans to visit Australia, including the immortal invitation to 'slip another shrimp on the barbie'.

Barry Humphries
Comedian who has portrayed various quintessentially Australian characters, including Dame Edna Everage and the repulsive Sir Les Patterson.

Kerri-Anne Kennerley
Perky veteran television presenter of lightweight morning variety shows.

Nicole Kidman
Hugely successful actor in both mainstream and art-house film roles. She won an Academy Award in 2003 for her portrayal of Virginia Woolf in *The Hours*.

Elle Macpherson
Former supermodel and now successful businesswoman, still sometimes referred to by her modelling nickname, 'The Body'.

Rove McManus
Popular presenter of television variety show *Rove Live*, which first aired in late 2000.

Ian 'Molly' Meldrum
Since hosting *Countdown*, his epoch-defining music show of the 1970s and 80s, Molly has been an influential fixture of the music scene. Famously never seen without his cowboy hat.

>

<

Kylie Minogue
Singer/actor who got her break in the soap opera *Neighbours* and has gone on to become one of the world's top-selling female artists. She was nicknamed the 'Singing Budgie' by critics early in her career.

Bert Newton
Nicknamed 'Moonface', Newton is a very popular and cheesy TV host – one of the originals of Australian television, having been in the limelight since the 1960s.

Shopping

In some countries shopping is what you do when you run out of necessities – but not in Australia, where for many folk shopping is just another way to occupy yourself. Try the following shopping terms on for size:

Akubra	a famous brand of Aussie hat
Australiana	the mass-produced trinkets found in souvenir shops, usually imported from Asia
bumbag	what Americans call a 'fanny pack' (note that in Australia, 'fanny' is vulgar slang for female genitalia, so if you insist on using 'fanny pack' be prepared for either gasps or giggles)
chemist	a pharmacy or pharmacist
daks	men's trousers; also used to describe tracksuit pants, as in *trackie daks*
Driza-bone	famous brand of Aussie oilskin raincoat
haberdashery	a shop that sells sewing supplies
handbag	a woman's carry bag – a 'purse' in North America
hire purchase	what Americans call 'installment buying'
lay-by	reservation of an item by payment of a deposit – not a roadside stopping place as in the UK

manchester	bed and bathroom linen
moleskins	jeans made of brushed cotton
nappy	known as a 'diaper' by North Americans
pram	a 'baby buggy' in North America
purse	known as a 'change purse' in North America
skivvy	long-sleeved turtleneck top made of stretch cotton
spanner	a 'monkey wrench' in the USA
stroller/pusher	small wheeled chair for small children, often called a 'pushchair' elsewhere
thongs	flip flops
vest	a sleeveless outer garment (not a 'singlet' as in the UK)

Festivals

Here are just a handful of the celebrations which are held around Australia.

AUSTRALIA DAY

On January 26, Australia commemorates the landing of the First Fleet in 1788 with a national holiday, concerts and other celebrations, and the announcement of the Australia Day Awards, including the award for Australian of the Year. A good occasion for a *barbie*!

BEER CAN REGATTA

This rowdy occasion in July/August is a 'sailing' race at Mindil Beach in Darwin between 'boats' built with empty beer cans – half the fun for the competitors is emptying the beer cans. For those who prefer activities on terra firma, there are bottomless boat races on sand, thong-throwing competitions and bathing beauty contests.

BARUNGA FESTIVAL

Attracting about 40 Aboriginal groups from all over the Northern Territory, this festival in early June is a great way to experience some Aboriginal culture. It's held at Barunga, 80km southeast of Katherine, and has traditional arts and crafts exhibits, native dancing, sports and music. You can sample Australian *bush tucker* too – honey ants, kangaroo, witchetty (*witjuti*) grubs and roasted *possum*, snake and *goanna* (a lizard).

HENLEY-ON-TODD REGATTA

A boat race on a dry river bed? Head for Alice Springs in late September to check out the crews 'wearing' their colourful, inventive boat creations as they stir up the dust – bounding for glory down the empty Todd River. And watch out for the *Camel Cup* in July when it's the camels' turn (without the seacraft) to compete in the same dry river bed.

MELBOURNE MOOMBA FESTIVAL

Running over four days in March, this summer festival ends with a street parade reigned over by the year's Moomba Monarch, usually a popular TV or sporting personality. The word *moomba* was thought to mean 'let's get together and have fun' in an Aboriginal language. In fact, a more accurate translation would be 'up your bum'.

SHINJU MATSURI

Around August, the port town of Broome celebrates its pearling history and diverse cultural heritage with Shinju Matsuri (the Pearl Festival). This colourful festival is launched by a traditional opening ball and finishes with a beach concert – Opera-under-the-stars – and a brilliant fireworks display, with must-see dragon boat races in between.

PORT FAIRY FOLK FESTIVAL

The usually low-key Victorian coastal town of Port Fairy welcomes a deluge of folk music fans every Labour Day weekend in March. As well as live music, the festival also presents a jam-packed programme of storytelling, music classes and singalongs, dancing, a food festival and street markets.

SYDNEY GAY & LESBIAN MARDI GRAS

Not just a famously spectacular parade and an all-night dance party in Oxford Street, this is a month-long festival in February that also features theatre, art, photography and music in a celebration of gay and lesbian life.

TAMWORTH COUNTRY MUSIC FESTIVAL

Yeehah! Tamworth is Australia's 'Country Music Capital' and each January, guitars, voices and award ceremonies entertain the booted throngs for around 10 days. Find a good perch on Peel Street when the cavalcade of floats, bands and line-dancers move through the town for the parade celebrating country music. Rodeos are also a big feature.

TORRES STRAIT CULTURAL FESTIVAL

In May every two years, Thursday Island hosts the Torres Strait Cultural Festival, designed to promote and strengthen the islands' cultural identity. Activities Include traditional dance, traditional and contemporary singing, and stalls selling food, handicraft and carvings.

BEANIE BEANO

Alice Springs celebrates the *beanie*, a popular winter headdress, in early July during the Beanie Festival. One of the big drawcards is the competition giving prizes like 'the craziest beanie' and 'the best made beanie'.

ROYAL SHOWS

Each city has a Royal Show offering livestock contests, agricultural displays, novelty rides and sideshows. The cake decorating competitions and the showing-off of primped and preened cats and dogs also (amazingly) draw people by the thousands. Kids find the 'showbags' containing chocolate, lollies, toys and other wares hard to resist. This is the place to gobble down *fairy floss*, *toffee apples* and *dagwood dogs*.

March/April	Royal Easter Show, Sydney
July	Royal Darwin Show, NT
August	Royal National Agricultural Show (the Ekka), Brisbane
August/ September	Royal Shows, Melbourne, Adelaide, Perth

B & S BALLS

Bachelors' & Spinsters' Balls – held in big tents and shearing sheds in rural areas all over Australia – attract the young and thirsty In their thousands. Alcohol is *skolled* in mind-blowing amounts by bachelors in black tie and spinsters in taffeta gowns.

FILM FESTIVALS

Celebrations of celluloid are held in each major city and showcase contemporary films from around Australia and the globe. The International Film Festival in Melbourne has long been regarded as Australia's best, offering film buffs fabulous cinema during the winter months of July and August. Short film festivals are also popular – check out Tropfest in Sydney or the St Kilda Film Festival in Melbourne.

ARTS FESTIVALS

There are various arts festivals staged around Australia that act as magnets for 'culture vultures' and give thousands of local and international artists an opportunity to wow audiences with their talents. On offer is an extraordinary range of opera, dance, drama, comedy, film, music, visual arts, literature and street parades, interspersed with plenty of parties.

Sydney Festival (January) kickstarted by a fireworks extravaganza above the Harbour Bridge on New Year's Eve

Perth International Arts Festival (February/March) the oldest, and one of the largest, of the arts festivals

Adelaide Festival of Arts (March, biennial) considered by many to be the most innovative of all the arts festivals. There's also an excellent 'alternative' festival called *Adelaide Fringe*.

Brisbane River festival (September) Brisbane's major festival of the arts, with buskers, concerts and other performances

Melbourne Festival (October) combines big-name Australian and international performers and visual artists. It's preceded in September by the *Melbourne Fringe Festival*, which focuses on new and 'innovative' art.

DESERT MOB

Every September the *Desert Mob* art show at the Araluen Centre in Alice Springs exhibits a diverse range of work from established and emerging Aboriginal artists from all over the Northern Territory, South Australia and Western Australia.

Parties

The party, otherwise known as *a bit of a bash* among older Australians, is central to the Australian expectation of having a good time in life. The typical party-goer can be spotted mingling in someone's backyard in shorts and a T-shirt or something similarly casual, waiting for meat – and also vegie burgers or seafood these days – to finish sizzling on a barbecue. The barbecue is often attended to by males, who seem to take unusually great pride in the wielding of metal tongs. Parties are also squeezed into everything from warehouse apartments to old flats. The old-fashioned *tinnie* is still a favourite with party-goers, but *stubbies*, wine and mixed drinks in a can (scotch and coke et al) also feature. Conversation can get fixated on certain topics such as sport.

Once upon a time in Australia, men at parties mostly just talked to other men (about sport and other blokey pursuits) and women to other women (about clothes and children of course). This still happens occasionally but parties now are much more likely to be all-in, intermingled affairs.

You might be invited to a *shindig*, *wing-ding*, *piss-up*, *booze-up* or *shivoo*, but don't fret that you're being asked to join a weird secret society – these are all words for a party. Once there, you may find yourself *making small talk*, *chewing the fat* or having a *chit-chat*, a *bit of a yarn*, a *gossip session*, a *natter* or a *yack* – in other words, a conversation. If you meet a like-minded soul you may even find yourself having a a *deep and meaningful* (*d&m*) conversation about life.

PARTY PROTOCOL

Before going to a party, head to the nearest bottle shop and buy whatever *poison* takes your fancy. This isn't a suggestion that suicide might be preferable to the party! *Poison* is drink – alcoholic drink.

PARTY FRIDGE

It's common to find the bathtub or laundry sink full of ice during parties. If you're happy to share your favourite *drop* (ie kind of alcohol) and sample what others have brought, put it there to chill. If not, find a safer place for it.

Most commonly, people either go to the party armed with **tinnies** which can be purchased in a **slab** (a carton of 24 cans of beer), or opt for the trusty cask of **plonk** (cheap wine, red or white). On arrival at the party, you'll **wet your whistle** with your first drink. Notice will have been given either verbally or in writing that the party is **BYO** (sometimes **BYOG**) – 'Bring Your Own (Grog)'. Sometimes barbecues will be labelled **BYOGM** – 'Bring Your Own Grog and Meat'. The host will then provide the extras.

For more drinking terms, see page 75.

While on the subject of protocol, many Australians still smoke, but don't light up a cigarette (*ciggie*, *fag* or *smoke*) in someone's home without asking them first if it's okay.

PISSED AS A FART

Judging by the following lists, some Australians must spend their time at parties thinking up new ways of describing their condition!

drunk

blotto	drunk as a skunk
faceless	full as a goog/boot
legless	off your face
paralytic	pickled
pissed as a fart/newt/parrot	pissed out of your brain
pissed to the eyeballs	plastered
primed	rat-arsed
shickered	sloshed
sozzled	stewed to the gills
tanked	tight as a tick

>

<

high

bombed	high
high as a kite	loaded
off the planet	ripped
smashed	spaced out
spacey	stoked
stoned	

throw up

chunder	do a technicolour yawn
drive the porcelain express	spew

NIBBLIES PROTOCOL

If you're asked to *bring a plate* to a party, function or barbecue, bring a plate of food (not an empty plate!) to share with the other guests. The hosts or organisers will sometimes ask you to bring something specific, to ensure that they don't end up with 20 plates of lamingtons on the table. If it's left to you to decide, choose your 'plate' to suit the occasion – generally, things like cakes, slices or biscuits, pies or sausage rolls, and dips, breads and antipasto-type *nibblies* will be appreciated.

LEAVING THE PARTY

On leaving a party, some common expressions include: *Cheerio, I'm going to choof (off) now*, and *I'm going to chuck it in for the night*. Those who can still talk the next day can admit to a hangover with symptoms described as *blue devils*, *the DTs*, *the horrors*, *the Joe Blakes* (shakes) and *pink elephants and dingbats*. This isn't necessarily to say that the sufferer is a heavy drinker or an *alkie*, *booze artist*, *booze-hound*, *grog artist*, *hard case*, *lush*, *pisshead*, *pisspot*, *soak* or *sponge*! Some may well be *two-pot screamers* – totally *off their heads* after just two beers.

Gambling

Australians appear to be addicted to gambling and are likely to bet on just about anything, including the likelihood of whether or not they'll bet on anything. One of the most popular forms of gambling is the coin operated device that elsewhere is known as a 'slot machine' but here is called a 'poker machine', *pokie* or a *one-armed bandit*. These machines used to be restricted to casinos and social clubs but nowadays have swamped many pubs as well.

Long before the advent of the poker machine, however, there was the game of *two-up*. A person known as the *spinner* – summoned into the middle of a ring with the call 'Come in spinner' – would hold a flat board called a *paddle* or *kip* on which two coins rested. The spinner would toss the coins into the air and gamblers would bet on whether the coins would land showing two heads or two tails – if the coins showed one head and one tail it would be deemed an *odd toss* and no money would be won or lost. The game is rarely seen nowadays, though some casinos still stage it.

Taking a punt (betting) on the *nags* (the horses) is probably the most popular form of gambling in Australia, particularly when horse racing carnivals or major events such as the Melbourne Cup (see page 136) are being held. Nowhere near as high profile as horse racing but still popular are the *dogs* (greyhound racing).

A more discreet form of gambling takes place in newsagents which sell *scratchies* – lottery tickets that have panels you scratch off with a coin to potentially reveal a prize underneath.

SILLY VERSUS SERIOUS

'Ladies and gentlemen, the match is about to begin. In my left corner, the famous *Australian comedy*, with a proud history from the *Dad and Dave* days of the 1930s through to my personal favourite, *Kath & Kim*. And in my right, the one, the only, *Australian drama*! A heavy-hitter, this one – watch out for the deadly Peter Weir uppercut and Geoffrey Rush right hook …'

Australians love to laugh at themselves, and as a result the Australian film and television archives are stuffed with comedies playing up the idiosyncrasies of the nation. These tend to be what the rest of the world thinks of when Australian film or TV is mentioned:

- *The Adventures of Priscilla, Queen of the Desert*
- *The Castle*
- *Crackerjack*
- *Crocodile Dundee*
- *Kath & Kim*
- *Muriel's Wedding*
- *Strictly Ballroom*

Less instantly recognisable as Australian, but equally weighty in number and accolades are the 'serious' Australian offerings, including gems such as:

- *Bad Boy Bubby*
- *Breaker Morant*
- *Chopper*
- *Dark City*
- *Dead Calm*
- *Japanese Story*
- *Lantana*
- *The Proposition*
- *Rabbit-proof Fence*
- *Romper Stomper*
- *Shine*
- *Somersault*
- *Wolf Creek*

If you're a visitor to Australia, you may be puzzled by hearing a red-headed person nicknamed *Blue* or *Bluey*. Then there's *feeling blue* meaning 'feeling depressed', *making a blue* meaning 'making a mistake', *picking a blue* meaning 'starting a fight or argument', *copping a bluey* meaning 'receiving a traffic infringement notice', *watching a blue movie* meaning 'watching a pornographic film' and *the boys in blue* meaning 'the police'.

The word *crook* is another minefield – there's *feeling crook* meaning 'feeling sick', *eating something crook* meaning 'eating something likely to cause food poisoning', *being crook at/with someone* meaning 'being angry with them', *being a crook* meaning 'being a swindler or a thief' and *something being crook* meaning 'something being illegal or broken'.

Confused? Welcome to the Australian colloquialism.

Doing things

bag	criticise
bludge	laze around, evade responsibilities
bored shitless	be extremely bored
bung	put, as in 'Just bung it in the oven'
cark it	collapse or die
chuck a berko	express extreme anger
come a cropper	fall over, have an accident or fail
cream	defeat decisively
dip your lid	show respect for someone or something
fart-arse around	waste time
feel like a shag on a rock	feel alone, deserted, forlorn, left out
front up	present yourself, make an appearance

get a guernsey	succeed or win approval (originally to be selected for a football team – a *guernsey* is a football jumper)
get stuck into somebody	criticise someone
give a bum-steer	mislead someone
give it a burl	try
hang out for	anticipate eagerly
have a shot at it	try
have tickets on yourself	have an inflated opinion of your own worth
lash at it	try
live on the smell of an oily rag	live frugally
muck around	fool around

pick the eyes out of it	take all the best bits
play funny buggers	be silly or behave dishonestly
pull a swiftie	do something dishonest or unfair
pull your head in	mind your own business
rapt	enthusiastic or happy (enraptured)
rubbish (someone)	pour scorn on
see a man about a dog	do something secretively – usually going to the toilet
shoot through	die or leave (quickly)
skite	boast
spill your guts	reveal a secret or your feelings
stick your bib in	interfere
stir the possum	tease and/or deliberately cause trouble
strike a blow	help with something (eg housework)
swing the billy	put the kettle on with the intention of making a cup of tea
tee up	arrange something (eg a meeting)
wag	skip school without permission

People

Someone who *couldn't organise a piss-up in a brewery* is very disorganised, but if there are *no flies on him/her* the person is clever, alert and can't easily be fooled. Others *would come to the opening of an envelope* (that is, they're social climbers and/or party addicts who will come to any party or function), but *wouldn't shout if a shark bit them* (are too stingy to buy drinks for others). And some people you just *don't know from a bar of soup* – you've never met them before.

People can also be described as being *born in a tent* (having a tendency to leave doors open), being *lower than a snake's belly/armpits* (very mean, cruel or dishonest), being *rough as guts* (very rough, uncivilised or rude) or being *rooted*, *stuffed* or *zonked* (exhausted). Here are some more terms:

anklebiter	child
bloke	man – but the American term 'guy' is increasingly used instead
blow-in	unexpected or uninvited guest
bludger	someone who does no or very little work
blue heeler	police officer (from the name of a breed of Australian cattle dog)
bogan	someone (usually working-class and urban) considered to lack style and sophistication
checkout chick	supermarket checkout clerk
curly	nickname for a bald person
fruit loop	silly or crazy person ('fruit loops' are a sugary breakfast cereal)
hoon	a young man who drives fast and/or recklessly
Joe Blow/Bloggs	the average citizen, any man
larrikin	either a cheeky and irreverent person or a lout (old-fashioned)
mate	friend
no-hoper	a loser, someone very incompetent
old cheese	mother
poofter	homosexual man (offensive)

quack	doctor (can be contemptuous)
rug rat	child
shitkicker	someone who does all the menial or unpopular jobs
tacker	child
tight-arse	stingy person
wally	fool, idiot
wanker	idiot and/or someone pretentious

Places & objects

You might have *more of something than you could poke a stick at* (a lot of it) in which case you'd probably be happy to give it away. On the other hand, if you would like something returned, tell the borrower it's a *boomerang*!

Places or things can also be:

all the go	fashionable
as scarce as hen's teeth	very rare
as useful as a glass door on a dunny	useless
cactus	broken or useless
cheap as chips	very cheap
chock-a-block	completely full
chockers	full (from 'chock-a-block')
cruddy	poor quality
not worth a brass razoo	not worth anything
not worth a crumpet	worthless
on the nose	very smelly
o.s.	overseas
skewiff	askew
squiffy	askew or tipsy
wonky	unstable, unsteady

Here are a few other colloquialisms you might be puzzled by:

blower/rap-rod	telephone
idiot box	television
pong	bad smell
poo tickets	toilet paper
shrapnel	small-denomination coins
stormstick	umbrella
thingo	a thing; also a *doovelacki*, *thingamajig* or *whatchamacallit*

Actions & situations

Aussie salute	the action of brushing flies away from your face
belter	really good, as in 'It was a belter'
bingle	car accident
blind Freddy	used to point out how obvious something is, as in 'Even blind Freddy would see that'
cooking with gas	something going well and as planned
crust	a living, as in 'What do you do for a crust?'
dead cert/set	absolutely certain
fizzer	a failure, disappointment, as in 'The party was a real fizzer'
flat chat/out	doing something very quickly
flat out like a lizard drinking	very busy
get a wriggle on	hurry up
grouse	good
hang on a tick/sec	wait a moment
in strife	in difficulties (not necessarily arguing or fighting)
in two shakes of a lamb's tail	in very short amount of time

not even in the race for it	having no hope of achieving a goal
piece of piss	easy task
playing pocket billiards	man adjusting his genitals
prang	car accident
Rafferty's rules	no rules at all, very disorganised
Rattle your dags!	Hurry up!
Reckon!	You bet!
ron	later (a contraction of 'later on')
r.s.	lousy (short for 'ratshit')
rug up	dress warmly
she'll be apples	everything will be okay
she's sweet	as for *she'll be apples*
spewing	literally, vomiting – but often used to mean 'upset' or 'disappointed'
stinker	a very hot day
Too right!	yes, most definitely, of course
wog	virus or stomach upset; derogatory term for someone of Mediterranean or Middle Eastern extraction
yonks	a long time, as in 'I haven't seen Thommo for yonks'

BUCKLEY'S, MATE!

If somebody tells you that you have *Buckley's*, *Buckley's chance* or *Buckley's and none*, they're saying you have little or no chance. This expression refers in part to convict William Buckley, who managed to escape from the Port Phillip Bay penal colony in 1803 and was considered to have no chance of surviving. (In fact, he ended up living with the Aboriginal people of the present-day Geelong area for over 30 years before being rediscovered by the authorities.) The expression only became fully formed after *Buckley's chance* became tied to a pun on the name of a Melbourne department store which opened in 1851, Buckley and Nunn – hence, *Buckley's and none*.

'Like a ...'

The little expression *like a ...* opens a world of possibilities in Australian slang. A few of the more well-known or remarkable comparisons follow.

like a cocky on a biscuit tin   left out, not included. Used after Arnotts chose a colourful parrot rather than a sulphur-crested cockatoo to become part of their logo.

like a dunny in a desert   standing out, very conspicuous

like a moll at a christening   extremely out of place and uncomfortable

like a rat up a drain pipe   very quick, restless and erratic

like a rooster one day and a feather duster the next   very important, special and useful one moment and very un-important and common the next

like a stunned mullet   in a state of complete confusion, astonishment or inertia. The mullet, being a large fish, is knocked over the head after it's been caught, and as it's a common fish to catch perhaps its dazed expression has become familiar.

Other *like a ...* expressions include:

charge like a wounded bull   charge outrageously high prices

feel like a grease spot   feel hot and sweaty

go down like a lead balloon   be a complete failure

go through (someone) like a dose of salts   have a laxative effect. Of a person, be very angry with someone.

looks like a dog's breakfast   is in a dreadful mess

need (something) like a hole in the head   don't need it at all *running around like a headless chook* making a lot of commotion but not getting anywhere – the ultimate in pointless activity! It refers to the farmyard scene where the *chook* (chicken) intended for the day's dinner gets its head cut off. If it's not held down, sometimes the headless *chook* runs around until the message finally gets through to its body that it's dead.

FEELINGS

To describe how they're feeling, Australians often bypass the simple adjectives (happy, sad, etc) for creative, if not down-right bizarre, imagery. Here are a few examples:

anger
mad as a cut snake
mad as a frilled lizard
mad as a maggot
mad as a meataxe

crudeness
rough as a goat's knees
rough as a pig's breakfast
rough as bags

dryness
dry as a bone
dry as a chip
dry as a dead dingo's donger
dry as a nun's nasty
dry as a pommy's towel

fitness
fit as a Mallee bull

fullness
full as a boot
full as a bull's bum
full as a footy final
full as a goog (ie an egg)
full as a state school hat rack
full as a tick
full to pussy's bow

>

<

happiness
happy as a dog with two tails
happy as Larry

insanity
has a few kangaroos loose in the top paddock
mad as a gumtree full of galahs
mad as a mother-in-law's cat
off your rocker
off your scone
silly as a bagful of worms
silly as a wheel

sadness
happy as a bastard on Father's Day
miserable as a bandicoot
miserable as a shag on a rock

uselessness
useful as a pocket on a singlet
useful as a sore arse to a boundary rider
useful as a third armpit
useful as tits on a bull

weakness
weak as piss
weak as water
weaker than a sunburned snowflake

'Short of a ...'

Australians often use *short of a ...* phrases to talk about someone who seems a bit stupid or mentally unstable. Occasionally you might hear someone described as:

a book short of a library *a can short of a slab*
an egg short of a dozen *a grape short of a bunch*
a penny short of a pound *a sandwich short of a picnic*
a snag short of a barbie *a stubby short of a sixpack*

Rhyming slang

Rhyming slang was borrowed from Cockney English, and then added to in Australia. Some Australians seem to enjoy using it to spice up their conversation, but don't worry if you find it confusing – the community as a whole operates successfully without it.

after darks	sharks
aristotle	bottle
babbling brook	cook
Bob Hope	soap
Captain Cook	look
cheese and kisses	missus (wife)
comic cuts	guts
dead horse	sauce, usually tomato sauce
dog and bone	phone
hammer and tack	back
hey-diddle-diddle	piddle
hit-and-miss	piss
Jimmy Britts	shits
Jimmy Dancer	cancer
Joe Blake	snake
Noah's ark	shark
on one's Pat Malone	alone
optic nerve	perve (look)
Richard the Third	turd
steak and kidney	Sydney
tom(my) tits	shits

amster – Amsterdam ram
An old-fashioned word for a person who tries to drum up business outside a sideshow. 'Amsterdam ram' is a British word for the same kind of showman, also known as a *drummer*, *spruiker* or *urger*.

barmaid's blush – a flush (in poker)
Also refers to a drink made from port wine and lemonade, or rum and raspberry.

***Barry Crocker** – a shocker*
A poor performance.

***butcher's (hook)** – look*
As in 'Have a butcher's at this', not to be confused with:

***butcher's (hook)** – crook*
Feeling sick. When you have the *lurgi* (some vague unidentifiable illness, usually one that's going around), then you 'feel butcher's'.

***china (plate)** – mate*
Old-fashioned word for a friend.

***Dad and Dave** – shave*
'Dad and Dave' was a well-known radio show during the 1930s, 40s and 50s.

***frog and toad** – road*
As in 'Let's hit the frog'n'toad!'

***loaf (of bread)** – head*
'Use your loaf' is an encouragement to think.

***onka (paringa)** – finger*
Onkaparinga is also the name of a brand of woollen blanket.

***reginalds (Reg Grundies)** – undies*
Underwear. Reg Grundy was a well-known TV entrepreneur. *Reginalds* are also known as *reggies*.

***scarper (Scapa Flow)** – go*
Go away, usually at high speed or with some urgency.

***septic (tank)** – Yank*
An American. Also shortened to *seppo*.

***titfer (tit for tat)** – hat*
Another term for hat is *this-an'-that*.

***warwick (Warwick Farm)** – arm*
Named after a well-known racecourse in Sydney.

LOOK WHO'S TALKING

To have a gander doesn't mean 'to eat a goose', it means 'to look at' and so do these phrases:

bo-peep	'Take a bo-peep at that bloke.'
geezer	'Ey, have a geezer at that.'
perve	to look at lustfully
squizz	'Hey, cop a squizz at this!'
sticky beak	to look, usually uninvited, as in 'I had a sticky beak at the neighbour's new pool when they were out.'

There are also quite a few ways to describe incessant talk, including:

chew someone's ear off	**ear bash**
flap the gums	**raving on**
talk someone blind	**talk the leg off a chair**
verbal diarrhoea	**yacking**
yapping	

Abbreviations & acronyms

AAP	Australian Associated Press
ABC	Australian Broadcasting Corporation (nicknamed 'Auntie')
ACF	Australian Conservation Foundation
ACT	Australian Capital Territory
ACTU	Australian Council of Trade Unions (pronounce each letter)
AFI	Australian Film Institute
AFL	Australian Football League
ALP	Australian Labor Party
AMA	Australian Medical Association
ANU	Australian National University (Canberra)
ANZAC	Australian and New Zealand Army Corps (pronounced 'anzak')

ASIO	Australian Security Intelligence Organisation (pronounced 'ayzeeoh')
ASIS	Australian Secret Intelligence Service
ASX	Australian Stock Exchange
ATO	Australian Taxation Office
CHOGM	Commonwealth Heads of Government Meeting (pronounced 'chogum')
C of E	Church of England
CPI	Consumer Price Index
CSIRO	Commonwealth Scientific & Industrial Research Organisation
CST	Central Standard Time (the time zone of South Australia and the Northern Territory – GMT+9.5)
CWA	Country Women's Association
EFTPOS	Electronic Funds Transfer at Point Of Sale (payment by bank transfer in shops)
EPA	Environment Protection Authority
EST	Eastern Standard Time (the time zone of all eastern states in Australia – GMT+10)
GG	Governor-General
GPO	General Post Office
GST	Goods & Services Tax
HMAS	Her Majesty's Australian Ship
HSC	Higher School Certificate
MCG	Melbourne Cricket Ground
MP	Member of Parliament
NGA	National Gallery of Australia
NIDA	National Institute of Dramatic Art (pronounced 'naidah')
NRMA	National Roads & Motorists' Association (of New South Wales)
NSW	New South Wales
NT	Northern Territory
ONO	or nearest offer
OYO	own your own apartment
PAYG	pay as you go (tax)
PIN	Personal Identification Number
Qld	Queensland
RAAF	Royal Australian Air Force

RACV	Royal Automobile Club of Victoria
RACQ	Royal Automobile Club of Queensland
RAN	Royal Australian Navy
RBA	Reserve Bank of Australia
RRP	Recommended Retail Price
RSL	Returned & Services League (of Australia)
RSPCA	Royal Society for the Prevention of Cruelty to Animals
RWC	Road Worthy Certificate (the safety check required before a car is bought or sold in Victoria)
SA	South Australia
SCG	Sydney Cricket Ground
SBS	Special Broadcasting Service – TV and radio station and online service, focusing on multicultural programmes
STA	State Transit Authority (NSW)
STD	Subscriber Trunk Dialling (you need to use STD codes when dialling numbers outside local zones)
TAFE	Technical & Further Education (pronounced 'tayf')
Tas	Tasmania
VFA	Victorian Football Association
Vic	Victoria
WA	Western Australia
WRAAF	Women's Royal Australian Air Force
WRAN	Women's Royal Association Navy
WST	Western Standard Time (the time zone of Western Australia – GMT+8)
YHA	Youth Hostels Association (known worldwide as Hostelling International)
YMCA	Young Men's Christian Association
YWCA	Young Women's Christian Association

COBBER

The word *cobber*, an old-fashioned Aussie word for 'friend', stems from 'to cob' meaning 'to take a liking to someone', originally from a Suffolk dialect of the 1800s.

SLANG

MISUNDERSTANDINGS

Despite the spirit of sharing that exists between Australian English and other forms of English, there are numerous instances of disagreement over which word to use. Following are some of the most common examples.

American English

Australian English	American English
barrack for	root for
bonnet	car hood
boot	trunk
braces (for trousers)	suspenders
camp bed	cot
capsicum	(bell) peppers
cot	crib
cyclone	hurricane
fairy floss	candy floss
fringe (hair)	bangs
ground floor	first floor
lollies	candy
takeaway	takeout
torch	flashlight
university	college

British English

Australian English	British English
bank teller	cashier
bushwalking	walking/hiking
doona	duvet

American English

Australian English	British English
eggplant	aubergine
freeway	motorway
garbo	dustman
highway	dual carriageway
icy pole/iceblock	(ice) lolly
lollies	sweets
overseas	abroad
paddock	field
private school	public school
public holiday	bank holiday
wharfie	docker
windcheater	sweatshirt
zucchini	courgette

New Zealand English

Australian English	New Zealand English
abattoir/slaughterhouse	freezing works
bitumen road	tarseal road
bushwalking	tramping
doona	duvet
esky	coolie bin
gravel/dirt road	metal road
holiday home	bach/crib (mainly Otago)
milk bar	dairy
speed humps/bumps	judder bars
thongs/sandals	jandals
uni	varsity (still heard in the UK as well, but mainly for Oxford and Cambridge)

There are two schools of thought about linguistic variations in Australia. One school suggests that different regional dialects are emerging, the other says that Australian English is generally the same across the country. Both schools are partly right. There's increasing evidence of regional differences, but compared to other English-speaking countries these are few and minor. This might seem surprising considering the large distances between most Australian cities, but the country was settled mainly along the coast within a rather short period and the mix of origins in the various cities was apparently fairly similar.

The most obvious regional differences involve vocabulary, and even those who stress linguistic uniformity admit there are quite a few of these. The regionalists, however, claim difference not just in the words we use but also in the way they are pronounced. It's claimed that a Melburnian can be distinguished from a Sydneysider, that everyone can tell a Queenslander, and that the South Australians can be picked as soon as they say 'school'. There are indeed differences in pronunciation (for more on pronunciation see page 22) but like most of the vocabulary differences these mainly involve tendencies rather than absolute contrasts. The differences are nowhere near as major as those which separate an Australian from a New Zealander, who simply has to ask for 'fush and chups' to be identified and whose English is travelling further along its own track with each generation.

The table on the following two pages gives a few of the terms which differ from state to state.

DIFFERENT STANDARDS

While there may be many Perth dwellers who have never called a swimming costume 'bathers' and many Brisbanians

	NSW	QLD	SA
10oz glass of beer	middy	middy	schooner
children's playground equipment for sliding down	slippery dip; slide	slippery dip	slippery dip; slide
a common black-and-white bird	magpie; peewee	magpie; peewee	Murray magpie; peewee
costume worn when swimming	cozzie; togs	togs	bathers; togs
fizzy drink with a dollop of ice-cream	ice-cream soda	ice-cream soda	spider
mid-morning break at primary school	playlunch; recess	little lunch; recess	playtime
non-alcoholic carbonated sweet drink	soft drink	cordial	soft drink
paste made from ground roasted peanuts	peanut butter	peanut paste	peanut butter
round slice of potato covered in batter and deep-fried	potato scallop	potato scallop	potato fritter
rubber loop used to hold small objects together	rubber band	rubber band	lacky band
small red sausages at cocktail parties	cocktail frankfurts	cheerios	frankfurts

that never call them 'togs', the following terms are generally typical of the different states:

TAS	VIC	WA
pot	pot	pot
slide	slide	slippery dip
magpie; mudlark	magpie; mudlark	magpie
bathers; togs	bathers; togs	bathers; togs
spider	spider	ice-cream soda
playtime	playlunch	recess
cordial	soft drink	soft drink
peanut butter	peanut butter	peanut butter
potato cake	potato cake	potato cake
rubber band	lacker band	rubber band
saveloys; little boys	cocktail sausages	frankfurts

Australian Capital Territory

The Australian Capital Territory is the small area of land surrounding the country's capital, Canberra.

ABOUT CANBERRA

Canberra has the feel of a big country town. It's a unique blend of town, gown (ie academia) and public service, full of politicians who zap in for the season in Parliament, and zap out again as fast as their planes can carry them.

The name 'Canberra' is thought to be the Aboriginal name for the area, meaning something like 'meeting place'. Walter Burley Griffin (1876–1937) created the original design of the city, and people are still divided about it. Almost everyone says they immediately get lost in Canberra's many roundabouts. (Those spending weary hours attempting to escape the endless loops and whirls have been known to hurl abuse at Griffin!)

ACT LINGO

bush week   the name for end-of-term student celebrations at the Australian National University

govie/guvvie home   a government-funded residence, usually offering low rent. An ***ex-govie*** is one of these residences being offered on the open market.

govie/guvvie school   a government-funded school ('state school' elsewhere)

New South Wales

New South Welshmen have sometimes been called ***cornstalks***. It seems that quite early in colonial days the climate and way of life agreed with the newcomers, and the men who grew up in Australia became noted for their height and slim build. They grew like cornstalks, with the body characteristically tapering from broad shoulders to slim hips.

ABOUT SYDNEY

Sydney has the Harbour Bridge, the Opera House, one of the world's finest harbours and a generally hedonistic climate. This leads some Sydneysiders to believe that Sydney is 'where it's at' and that all other Australian cities are urban irrelevancies. This point of view is of particular irritation to some Melburnians, mainly because said Melburnians believe that *their* city is the hub of Australian life. The parochialism of both cities tends to annoy everyone else in the country.

Sydney was named after Thomas Townshend, 1st Viscount Sydney, by Governor Arthur Phillip (1738–1814), the British naval officer who brought the First Fleet to Sydney Cove. Townshend was Secretary of the Home Department at the time.

As well as naming the city, Governor Phillip is the first person to have recorded the term *gum tree* for a eucalypt in his journal of 1789. The name was considered apt because the substance oozing from the tree was thought to be a kind of gum. Fifty years afterward it's clear that the colony had not only identified gum trees but knew what it was like to be up them. In the Australian context, *up a gum tree* came to mean 'in a state of confusion' or 'in a hopeless predicament' (a reference to the state of an animal trapped up a tree). The first recorded example of the phrase was a settler commenting on the behaviour of his workforce: 'My convicts were always drinking rum, I often wished they were up a gum tree.' (Some would say workplace relations in Australia have struggled to rise from this low point.)

ROSELLA JAM

A woman moved from Queensland, where a *rosella* is a type of fruit, to northern New South Wales, where it's a type of bird. She asked a local if he could get her some rosellas, and he enquired whether two would suffice – he was understandably surprised when she said she'd need more, as she wanted to make jam!

NEW SOUTH WALES LINGO

the Coathanger an irreverent name for the Harbour Bridge

Pitt Street farmer a city businessman who channels money into country property – he stereotypically wears a suit during the week and moleskins and workboots on the weekends

shoot through like a Bondi tram when Sydney had trams, there was one that went to Bondi Beach. Apparently there was a stretch of the track near Centennial Park when the tram picked up speed. Nowadays, to **shoot through like a Bondi tram** is basically to leave very quickly.

up the Cross if Bondi Beach represents everything that's fine in life, then King's Cross stands for everything that's sinful. These days it's a little outclassed by Oxford Street, but to go **up the Cross** is still to enter a gritty, down-at-heel world.

Northern Territory

The inhabitants of the Northern Territory are known as **Territorians**, naturally enough, or **Top Enders**.

ABOUT DARWIN

Darwin was named after Charles Darwin, the English naturalist, who visited Australia aboard HMS Beagle in 1836. Darwin has always been a multicultural city, funnelling traffic between the islands and peninsulas of Asia to Australia's Top End. This has resulted in some excellent Asian food markets, particularly on Mindil Beach, and meant that Darwin folk were eating laksa (Chinese-Malay noodle soup) for years before it appeared on menus in Sydney and Melbourne.

NORTHERN TERRITORY LINGO

the Wet   the monsoon season

the Dry   the opposite of the Wet. The final stage of this is referred to as **the build-up** (to the Wet) and is notorious for causing great irritability among inhabitants.

Darwin rig or **Territory rig**   a style of casual dress for men that's suitable for the humid conditions of the Top End, usually a short-sleeved, open-neck shirt and trousers. **Territory formal** means a long-sleeved shirt and tie – no jacket required. You'll often see these terms written at the bottom of invitations.

Queensland

Nicknamed 'the Sunshine State', Queensland certainly has more than its fair share of warm rays, and its coast attracts holidaymakers from all over Australia. However, inland Queensland, stretching up towards Cape York, is as tough a strip of outback as you could encounter. Towards the north is a region called the Channel Country in which numerous interlocking rivers regularly flood to form an inland sea.

Queensland is known as **Bananaland** and its inhabitants as **Bananabenders**, because of the big banana plantations on its southeastern coast.

ABOUT BRISBANE

Brisbane was established as a convict settlement for the worst offenders, and was celebrated in song as a place of ultimate despair. The city was named after Sir Thomas Brisbane, who was governor of New South Wales from 1821 to 1825. Notwithstanding this grim past, it has a reputation as a rather hedonistic city – steamy in summer but with a beautiful, clear, sunny winter to compensate.

QUEENSLAND LINGO

duchess   dressing table

the Gabba   the Brisbane Cricket Ground, so called because of its location in the suburb of Woollongabba

port   a suitcase – short for 'portmanteau'

Schoolies' Week   the rowdy end-of-year festivities for high school graduates after their final exams, usually centred on the Gold Coast

windsor sausage   a type of processed meat, sold as **devon**, **fritz** and **polony** in other states

South Australia

There are a lot of wide open spaces in South Australia – 1% of the population inhabits a whopping 80% of the state's land. As well as being home to some of Australia's leading wine districts, South Australia can claim to be the only Australian colony never to have admitted convicts.

South Australians are occasionally known as **Croweaters** – supposedly because life was so hard in the state that the colonials would be forced to eat crows.

ABOUT ADELAIDE

Adelaide is a pleasant town, well-heeled and respectable, as easy to live in as a country town and as interesting as an international city. It's named after Queen Adelaide, the wife of William IV, and is also known as the **City of Churches**. Its biggest claim to fame is probably the Adelaide Festival of Arts, a biennial affair which draws local and international talent.

SOUTH AUSTRALIAN LINGO

donkey   to give someone a ride on the back of your bike, what other Australians would refer to as either a *dink* or a *dinky*

fritz   also known as *bung fritz*, this is the South Australian word for *devon* – processed sandwich meat. It's a German term, brought to the state by the strong German community near Adelaide.

Stobie pole   kind of telegraph pole made of concrete and steel, named after its creator, JC Stobie

Tasmania

Tasmanians feel they are often overlooked by the rest of Australia – which they refer to as *the Mainland*, the inhabitants being *Mainlanders*. And certainly something seems to get lost in the translation over Bass Strait, so that Tasmania and the rest of Australia are never quite on the same wavelength.

Tasmania is also called the *Apple Isle*, a name that refers to the island's past success in growing apples; the inhabitants are sometimes referred to as *Apple Islanders*. *Tassie* is an affectionate shortening of the name *Tasmania*, while *Taswegian* is a common name for a Tasmanian.

ABOUT HOBART

Hobart is the second oldest city in Australia – the second convict settlement was established there in 1804. The city has an old-world charm: a fishing village character marked by docks and Georgian houses, with Mount Wellington towering above it. It was named after Robert Hobart, fourth Earl of Buckinghamshire and Secretary of State for War and the Colonies (1801–04). A rivalry exists between Hobart and Launceston which is similar to the tension between Sydney and Melbourne. Whatever Hobart does, Launceston has to equal or do better.

TASMANIAN LINGO

chalet an outhouse or small dwelling in the garden of a house

mutton bird a species of shearwater which nests on islands off Tasmania and is considered a gourmet meal, though it's extremely oily

Victoria

Victoria was once known as *the Cabbage Garden* because of the state's early ability to produce fruit and vegetables from its rich soil and accommodating climate. Victorians therefore were referred to as *Cabbage Gardeners*, the implication being that that's all they were good for. Victorians are also described as *Mexicans*, because from the point of view of New South Wales they are 'south of the border'.

ABOUT MELBOURNE

Melbourne was named in 1837 by Governor Bourke after Lord Melbourne, the British prime minister at the time. Melbourne is more English in its appearance than any other Australian capital, and its residents claim to live stylishly – to dine and dress well, and to be as cultured and sophisticated as Sydney is flamboyant.

One of Melbourne's distinctive features is its trams. They provide a pleasant way to move around the city, although it can be a slow ride to the suburbs (the tram system was devised before speed meant everything). Watch out for the burgundy-coloured City Circle Tram, a free service that loops the city centre.

VICTORIAN LINGO

like Bourke Street very busy, usually referring to traffic. Bourke Street is one of the busiest thoroughfares in Melbourne's central business district.

the City Loop the collective name for the five train stations arranged around the edge of the CBD

hook turn a driving manoeuvre which is only done in Melbourne's CBD and terrifies the rest of Australia. To turn right at an intersection, a motorist pulls over to the left of the road and then crosses all lanes of traffic to complete the turn. The hook turn is designed to keep the tram tracks clear of cars waiting to turn.

has more front than Myer Is cheeky, not at all shy. Myer is a department store that originated in Melbourne.

the Tan a popular 4km jogging track around Kings Domain and the Royal Botanic Gardens

AT THE RACES

The Melbourne Cup, the country's biggest horse race, still brings the nation to an almost eerie halt on the first Tuesday of each November at 3.20pm. The combination of betting and stopping work for the 3.2km event seems to be irresistible. Held at the Flemington Racecourse since 1861, the event draws a curious mix of elegantly turned out society types and boisterous masses enjoying the chance to dress up. Most of the rest of the country joins Cup sweeps, choosing a horse at random and placing a bet for possibly the only time of the year. It's rare to find an Aussie, especially a Melburnian, who isn't having some sort of *flutter* (bet) on the horses on this day.

Western Australia

Western Australia is Australia's largest state, encompassing extremes of landscape and weather. As a result words like 'remote' and 'isolated' turn up everywhere, as in the terms *isolated child*, *isolated class*, *isolated school* and *isolated pharmacy*, or *remote posting*, *remote resident* and *remote site*.

West Australians are sometimes called *Sandgropers*, because most of the state is desert. (To 'sandgrope' is to walk in soft sand, a procedure that most people find tiring.) *Sandgroper* can be shortened to *Groper* – and *Gropers*, of course, live in *Groperland*. The state is also sometimes referred to as *Westralia*, so West Australians are also *Westralians*.

ABOUT PERTH

Perth is separated from Australia's southern states by the Nullarbor Plain (*Nullarbor* being derived from the Latin 'nulla arbor', meaning 'no tree'). It was named by Captain James Stirling after the city of the same name in Scotland.

On the whole, people in this remote city show few signs of feeling far-removed from the more populated bits of the country, and seem content with the beautiful city they have. West Australians refer to inhabitants of the east coast as *t'othersiders* and *Eastern Staters*.

WEST AUSTRALIAN LINGO

the doctor   the cool sea breeze which blows inland in the late afternoon. In Perth it's known as the *Fremantle doctor* because it blows into Perth from the direction of Fremantle.

Kal   what the locals call Kalgoorlie

Nyungar   a West Australian Aborigine. In a local Aboriginal language *nyungar* means 'man'.

Rotto   Rottnest Island

skimpy   a scantily clad barmaid

QUOKKAS

Alarmed by the number of what appeared to be huge rats on a sandy island 19km off the Western Australian coast, the Dutch explorer De Vlamingh named the island in their honour – Rottnest, literally 'Rat's Nest'. The animals weren't rats, of course, but the very cute *quokkas*, relatives of the wallaby.

Other regions

Alhough they're not states or territories, a few other regions in Australia have distinct identities – the Riverina, New England and the Gold Coast.

THE RIVERINA (& SUNRAYSIA)
The lifeline of the Riverina is the Murray River, which feeds off the waters from the Snowy Mountains and then flows all the way to St Vincent's Gulf in South Australia. The area known as Sunraysia is centred on Mildura, Victoria, and sprang up around an irrigation scheme developed in 1923 which made the dried fruit and wine industries of the region possible.

NEW ENGLAND
New England, northeast of Sydney, is the district which claims the university town of Armidale as its centre. It's a farming and mining district – the name 'New England' has to be seen as wishful thinking on the part of the settlers.

THE GOLD COAST
The strip of coastline just south of Brisbane is known as the Gold Coast. It's a tourist phenomenon – high-rises perched on the edge of the beach. Other sections of the coast have also been given names, including the Sunshine Coast (further north) and the Capricorn Coast (the coastline near Rockhampton).

The original inhabitants of Australia have been living on this continent for something like 50,000 years. When the British established the first European settlement in Australia at Sydney Cove in 1788, the newcomers originally called the older inhabitants 'natives' and later 'Aborigines' or 'Aboriginal people'. Recently the term 'Indigenous' has come into general use to replace 'Aboriginal', though the noun 'Aborigine' remains and 'Aboriginal' is retained in the name of various bodies such as the Australian Institute of Aboriginal and Torres Strait Islander Studies in Canberra. Some Aboriginal people prefer to use one of their own names for themselves, which differ from area to area. There's no indigenous term that covers all Aboriginal people – the term *Murri* is used in Queensland, *Nyungar* (or *Nyoongah* or *Noongar*) in the southwest of Western Australia, *Yolŋu* in northeastern Arnhem Land, *Koori* or *Koorie* in New South Wales and Victoria, and *Palawa* in Tasmania.

The size of the Aboriginal population at the time the first Europeans came to Australia is not known, but estimates range from 300,000 to over a million. The people were hunter-gatherers – that is, they lived by hunting animals and gathering various plant foods. Each person belonged to a land-owning group, typically a clan with its own distinctive speech. Often a group of neighbouring clans would have similar forms of speech and we could say that these clans spoke dialects of a particular language.

Indigenous languages

It's estimated that in 1788 there were about 250 different languages in Australia, each comprising several dialects. However, over the course of the next 100 years the British took over the whole of Australia and in the process many Aboriginal people died, either as a result of introduced diseases or through being deliberately shot or poisoned. In areas where fertile land attracted a denser pattern of European settlement, most of the Aboriginal population perished. Today there are no speakers left of the languages of Tasmania, Victoria and most of New South Wales. The only flourishing languages are to be found in the centre of the continent and along the north coast.

Up until the 1960s government policy was for Aboriginal people to be assimilated, and the white community had a negative attitude towards Aborigines, which induced feelings of shame in Aboriginal people and attempts by part-Aborigines to hide their Aboriginal ancestry. Since then things have changed. Nowadays Aboriginal people are proud of their ancestry, and those who are of part-Aboriginal and part-European descent – the majority in the southeast – identify strongly as Aboriginal and reject the notion of 'part-Aborigine'.

Language classifications

Most of the languages of the Australian mainland share a number of roots such as *nga* for 'I', *bu*- for 'hit' and *ma*- for 'do', and look as if they are related. However, some of the shared forms may be the result of borrowing from one language to another. It is interesting to note that when the first people settled in Australia, the continent included New Guinea and Tasmania, but there are few if any resemblances between the languages of the present-day mainland and those of Tasmania, New Guinea or anywhere else.

The mainland languages have been classified into a score or so 'families' on the basis of shared vocabulary. One family, Pama-Nyungan, covers all of the mainland except the Top End of the Northern Territory and the Kimberleys of Western

Australia. The word **Pama-Nyungan** was made from **pama** (man) in some of the Cape York languages and **nyunga** (man) in the Perth area.

Another way of classifying the languages is to distinguish between those that use suffixing and those that use prefixing. In the suffixing languages all affixes come at the end of the word, as in English with 'books' and 'slowly'. The prefixing languages have suffixes, but they also have pronoun prefixes on the verb (see the Structure section on page 145 for more). The Pama Nyungan languages are almost all in the suffixing class and almost all the other families of the Top End and the Kimberleys are in the prefixing class.

Sounds

In Europe, languages such as French, Italian, German and Polish use very different sounds and thus sound very different from one another. Most Aboriginal languages, however, use much the same set of sounds, so they sound very similar.

VOWELS

Many Australian languages have only three distinct vowels, namely *i* as in 'Mimi', *a* as in 'father' and *u*, which can sound like the vowel in 'Lou' or sometimes like the vowel in 'law'. In some languages there are long versions of these vowels as well – basically the same but held longer. The long sounds are written *aa*, *ii* and *uu*.

CONSONANTS

All Australian indigenous languages use the *ng* sound as in 'sing', but it is common for this sound to appear at the beginning of a word, and early recorders often failed to hear it altogether. Initial *ng* occurs in the word for 'I' in a number of languages – Kalkadoon *ngai*, for example. Certain sounds found in English don't occur, such as *s*, *z*, *sh*, *f*, *v* and *h*.

Another notable feature of Aboriginal languages is that there's normally no distinction between *p* and *b*, *t* and *d*, and *k* and *g*. This is part of the reason that the names of some groups and their languages are spelled in different ways. The Warlpiri people of the Northern Territory, for example, used to be referred to as *Walbiri*. This can be a problem when it comes to using reference books, particularly where the first sound is the one that can be spelled differently. The name of the original inhabitants of the Adelaide area, for instance, has been spelled both 'Gaurna' and 'Kaurna' (the latter is the community's choice).

There are usually two *r* sounds in Australian languages. One is like the *r* sound in English. It occurs in *mara*, a widespread word for 'hand'. The other is like the *r* sound of Scottish English and is made by flipping the tongue up towards the roof of the mouth or sometimes trilling it. This *r* sound is usually written *rr*. Australian languages also have 'r-coloured' sounds, pronounced in a similar way to how a typical American would say the *r* in the middle of words like 'mourner', 'warder' and 'surly'. The sound occurs, for example, as *rn* in *murnong* (the yam daisy of Victoria) and *rd* (or *rt*) as in *nardoo* (a kind of fern and the flour made from the spores of this fern) – this word is actually *ngardu* and comes from the languages of western New South Wales and neighbouring states. There is also an r-coloured *l* as in *warli*, the Kaurna word for 'hut', which has come into English as 'wurley'.

Some Australian languages have dental sounds (sounds made when the tongue is touching the teeth), written *th* (or *dh*), *nh* and *lh*. Sometimes an underline is used to indicate these sounds (underline is also used in some areas for the r-coloured sounds mentioned above). The Aboriginal *th* sounds a little like *th* in English 'this'. Dental *n* and dental *l* are so similar to ordinary *n* and *l* in English that they can be distinguished only with practice.

Another distinctive feature of Aboriginal languages is a set of 'y-coloured' sounds made by holding the tip of the tongue down behind the lower teeth while pronouncing sounds such as *n*, *l* and *t*. These sounds are often written with a *y*, as in *ny*, *ly* and *ty* (also written *tj*). The *ny* occurs in **bunya**, the Yagara name of a tall pine-like tree found in southeastern Queensland. This sound may also occur at the beginning of a word, as in **Nyungar**, the name of the language and people of southwestern Western Australia. The *ly* sound occurs in **Alyawarra**, the name of an Arandic language spoken in the south-eastern part of the Northern Territory. The *ty* (or *dy*) sound is rather like the *ch* sound or the *j* sound in English. It occurs in **dyarra**, the name of a type of eucalypt from Western Australia. The word has been borrowed from the Nyungar language into English as 'jarrah'.

Word stress

In most Australian languages the main stress falls on the first syllable of a word. In long words there tend to be weak stresses on alternate syllables, as in the Kalkadoon word for boomerang, 'yálkapàri' (stress on the two bolded letters).

Writing

Aboriginal people did not have a system of writing before Europeans arrived. The first Europeans to write down Aboriginal words used English spelling conventions, but English has no consistent way of representing vowel sounds. The letter *u*, for example, represents one sound in 'but' and another in 'put'. In the 20th century it became popular to use the International Phonetic Alphabet (IPA) in which the vowel letters *a*, *e*, *i*, *o* and *u* had the values they have in the words

'Mama', 'Ray', 'Mimi', 'Lolo' and 'Lulu' respectively, and where the letter *j* indicates a *y* sound as in the German *ja* 'yes'.

Recently there has been a swing away from using IPA, though *ŋ* (upper case *Ŋ*) for the *ng* sound has been kept in a few language names such as **Yolŋu** (the group of languages belonging to northeast Arnhem Land). However, it's not always clear which convention is being used, so pronunciation can be tricky, particularly with a name containing *j* or *u*. There is a language in the north of Western Australia that was previously spelled 'Djaru', but is now 'Jaru', and the *j* is pronounced as in 'jam'. By contrast, in the Top End language Kuniwinjku, the *j* is pronounced *y*, with the *nj* representing the sound found at the end of French words such as *ligne* or *Boulogne*. Similarly, the language of the Yorke Peninsula in South Australia used to be spelled 'Narangga', but the community have adopted the spelling 'Narungga', where the *u* is to be pronounced as in 'but'. The same has happened with Bundjalung, previously 'Bandjalang', a language of the NSW-Queensland border.

Vocabulary

In the past people believed, mistakenly, that Aboriginal languages had only a few words. In fact, like any language, they have thousands. Many of these words don't correspond directly to English words – they express concepts particular to Aboriginal culture.

A striking feature of Aboriginal vocabulary is that the words found in one language are usually quite different from those found in neighbouring languages and elsewhere. This means that if you learn one Aboriginal language, you don't have much of a headstart for learning a second one. However, there are a few words that are widespread. This core of words includes the following:

bina	ear	**bula**	two
mara	hand	**mili**	eye
nyina	sit; remain	**tjalayn**	tongue
tjarra	thigh	**tjina**	foot

Typical Aboriginal words have more than one syllable. They usually begin with a consonant and end with a vowel, and they don't normally contain awkward sequences of consonants that are hard to pronounce. The Arandic languages of central Australia are an exception, however – a number of Arandic artists with tongue-twisting names are represented in Australian art galleries. The following words are fairly representative of a typical Australian language:

barramundi	type of fish, especially *Lates calcarifer* (central Queensland coast)
boobialla	shrubs of the *Myoporum* genus (southeastern Tasmania)
corroboree	ceremony with singing and dancing (Dharuk, Sydney area)
wallaby	kangaroo-like animal (Dharuk, Sydney area)

Structure

Aboriginal languages characteristically use different endings (case suffixes) on nouns and adjectives to mark relations between words in a sentence. In the Kalkadoon language of the Mount Isa area, for instance, a suffix is used to mark the entity responsible for an action. In the following example the ending **-yu** is attached to the word **martu** (mother):

> **Martu-yu ngulurrmai thuku.**
> Mother grabs the dog.

To indicate that the dog grabbed mother, you would put the suffix **-yu** on **thuku** (dog). Because the suffix picks out the actor (ie who's doing the grabbing), the word order can be varied to show different degrees of emphasis. You could have the following order, for instance, which emphasises that it's the dog that's being grabbed:

> **Thuku ngulurrmai martu-yu.**
> Mother grabs the dog.

Here are two more endings: *-piangu* meaning 'from' and *-kunha* meaning 'to':

> ***Kanimaintjirr ingka Darwin-piangu Melbourne-kunha.***
> The policeman goes from Darwin to Melbourne.

The word ***kanimaintjirr*** means 'policeman'. Literally it's 'the one who ties up' – ***kanimai*** is 'tie up' and *-ntjirr* is a suffix like the *-er* in English words such as 'driver'. It's an interesting example of how the Kalkadoon people made up a word for the new concept of policeman.

The majority of Australian languages attach pronouns to the verb. In a suffixing language like Kalkadoon these are attached to the end of the verb. For example, 'They sent me to town' would be ***Town-kunha ngkai-ngi-na*** where ***ngkai*** is 'sent', *-ngi* is 'me' and *-na* is 'they'. In a prefixing language, these pronouns would be attached at the front of the verb. In Kunwinjku, for example, 'I see them' is ***Nga-ben-na*** where the prefix ***nga*** is 'I', ***ben*** is 'them' and ***na*** is the verb 'to see'. (For those who speak French, it's rather like ***Je les vois*** – the unstressed pronouns precede the verb.)

Across the north of the continent many of the prefixing languages tend to have very complex verbs that seem more like sentences than single words. In Tiwi, the language of Bathurst and Melville Islands, for instance, the English sentence 'He sent them a message' can be expressed as a single word ***yu-wuni-marri-wa-yangirri***, literally 'he-them-with-words-sent'.

New languages

As in other parts of the world where European colonisation and accompanying social disruption have taken place, creole languages have arisen in northern Australia. 'Broken' is a creole spoken in the Torres Strait, and 'Kriol' is a creole spoken by many Aboriginal people across the north of Australia.

The sound system of both Broken and Kriol tends to reflect the traditional sounds of Aboriginal languages. The vocabulary is largely of English origin, mixed with some words from the traditional languages, but the meanings of many of the English words have been changed to refer to traditional concepts and distinctions. For example, in English the word 'we' refers to the speaker and one or more other persons. Aboriginal languages usually have a number of words for 'we', distinguishing between 'we' meaning two people and 'we' meaning more than two, and differing if the addressee (you) is included. These distinctions are carried over into the creoles. In the Kriol of Roper River, for instance, various words have been adapted from English to form the pronouns – *yunmi* means 'we' in the sense of 'you and me', *mintupala* means 'we two (not including you)' and there are a number of words for 'we' covering more than two people. These include *wi*, *melapat* and *mipala*.

Although these new languages have developed, tragically more than half of the original 250 or so Aboriginal languages have lost their last full speakers, some quite recently. However, Aboriginal people all over Australia are showing great interest in preserving what they can of their languages and in trying to restore them from materials recorded during past generations. In many parts of Australia Aboriginal children are being taught the language that belongs to their particular area at school.

Talking with Aboriginal people

Some Aboriginal people in central and northern Australia speak standard Australian English. Others, especially those who speak another language as their first language, may use a different kind of English, often known as Aboriginal English (see the box on page 170). Aboriginal English uses mostly English words, but takes its grammar, sounds and most of its cultural meanings from Aboriginal languages.

Many travellers would be aware of how insulting it is to be spoken to in 'pidgin' by a fluent speaker of a language. Not to mention how frustrating it is when someone speaks to you in a loud voice – as if you were deaf, rather than unable to understand the language. It's important to remember this when talking to people who don't speak English as their first language. Speak slowly and clearly, but don't insult someone by using baby talk or a kind of pidgin language, and don't speak in a voice that's louder than your normal speaking voice.

QUESTIONS

Asking direct questions (especially 'why' questions such as 'Why aren't you coming?') is considered rude by many Aboriginal people. As a rule, Aboriginal people do not interrogate one other as English speakers tend to do, but rely on each other to be reasonably cooperative in communicating information. It's better to make suggestions or statements or to talk around the issue than to ask direct questions: if you want to know where the Language Centre is, for example, say something like 'I'm trying to find my way to the Language Centre.' Don't always expect exact replies to your questions, either. It's unlikely that you'll be given anything but the most public information by people that you've just met.

Don't embarrass people by asking questions about anything that could be considered private, or expect that someone has time to stop and answer all of your questions. Many Aboriginal people are tired of being harassed by non-Aboriginal people on a search for spiritual or cultural knowledge, but may be too polite to say so. If you're particularly interested in finding out more about Aboriginal culture, you may want to join a tour organised by Aboriginal people, or enrol in a language or cross-culture course run by organisations such as the Institute for Aboriginal Development (in Alice Springs and Tennant Creek, see www.iad.edu.au) or Papulu Apparr-kari in Tennant Creek (PO Box 1108, Tennant Creek, 0861).

GREETINGS

Most Australian languages don't have greetings like 'hello', although Aboriginal people are now accustomed to English speakers using greetings, and some languages have adopted greetings based on the English form. These are used mainly to greet non-Aboriginal people, especially those who have begun to learn the language. Speakers of Aboriginal languages don't use these terms when talking to each other – instead, they often refer to or address others using a relationship term such as 'mother's brother' or a 'skin' name (ie the name of the section of the language group they belong to – see page 155).

PLEASE & THANK YOU

Likewise, many Australian languages don't have words for 'please' or 'thank you'. These days, more and more people use the English 'thank you', but thanks is otherwise expressed in actions rather than words. If someone does something for you, you show your thanks by doing something for that person or a relative at a later date. Similarly, if someone gives you something, it's appropriate to give them or one of their relatives something in return at another time – whether it's money, material goods, knowledge or even friendship. If you want to learn something, give something in return. Tell a story or anecdote to hear a story. Don't be too serious, and don't be too surprised to find yourself the butt of a joke. Aboriginal people also tend to tolerate more silence in communication than the average westerner. If no one says anything for a few minutes, don't feel compelled to fill the silence. Be content to wait and listen.

NAMES & CONVERSATION

It's generally not polite to ask people their name, as many English speakers do, to start a conversation. Among adults, first names are used much less than in non-Aboriginal society. If you really want to know a person's name, ask someone else nearby. A better way of starting a conversation, though, is to refer to a recent local event, or perhaps to admire a child who's accompanying the person you're speaking to. The best way is to tell them where you're from, and ask them where they're from. Aboriginal people, both men and women, always take each other's hand in greeting, with a gentle grip. They will usually expect you to introduce yourself first.

It also isn't polite to talk to a mother-to-be or a father-to-be about the child they're going to have. Aboriginal women may talk among themselves about pregnancy, but questions or interest from a stranger about this topic are likely to embarrass people into an awkward silence.

It's both offensive and upsetting for many Aboriginal people in central and northern Australia to hear the name of a close relative or friend who has recently passed away. The deceased should not be referred to directly – instead, describe a close relative as having lost a son, daughter etc. If someone has the same name, or a name that sounds the same as that of a person who's just passed away, then they may be given a new name, or they may be referred to in English as 'no name', an expression which has equivalents in most Australian languages: *kwementyaye* (Arrernte), *kumanjayi* (Warlpiri) or *kunmanara* (Pitjantjatjara). It's also offensive to show photographs of a person who's recently passed away.

BODY & SIGN LANGUAGE

Many Aboriginal people use hand signs and gestures during both everyday conversation and ceremonies. These signs are not limited to the deaf community, but are used and understood by all speakers. As you walk around towns like Alice Springs or Darwin, you may be aware of people using handsigns to communicate with each other across long distances, like across a river or a busy road, or in other situations where talking or shouting is not practical.

Be aware that Aboriginal people don't use eye contact as much as non-Aboriginal people. There are times, in fact, when eye contact is extremely inappropriate – for example, in certain kin relationships or between men and women who don't know each other. If you're a woman, you may find it refreshing to be able to walk past a large group of men without receiving even a glance, let alone a whistle! It's very important not to embarrass people by staring. Remember that you may end up embarrassing yourself if your stares are interpreted as indicating sexual interest.

KINSHIP SYSTEMS & POLITENESS
The most important organising principle of Aboriginal society is the kinship system – every member of the community is part of a complex web of kin relations. The kinship system not only means that particular relationships entail certain rights and obligations, but also provides a safety net for Aboriginal people when they are in trouble. Even far from home, the web of connections means that a person will be able to find a 'brother' or 'sister', a friend who will look after them. Aboriginal people travel a lot, and in some states such as Western Australia can expect nearly always to be close to 'family'.

The kinship system determines various patterns of social responsibility, many of which require special forms and styles of speaking. Thus there are rules of politeness and avoidance – traditionally, people would avoid their in-laws or use a special vocabulary when speaking in their presence. Children defer to members of their parents' generation, but interaction between members of the same generation, or between grandparents and grandchildren, is more relaxed and often involves a great deal of joking, teasing and innuendo.

Visitors can show consideration for these rules of politeness by treating older people with respect and reserve and by understanding that, in turn, younger people may treat them with reserve out of simple courtesy, not out of lack of friendliness.

RESTRICTIONS

As in most cultures, some knowledge is restricted and cannot be discussed freely. Certain rituals and particular sites, songs, dances and language styles may be restricted. Some objects, decorations or graphic designs may also be restricted and cannot be seen by uninitiated men and women.

All Aboriginal sites are protected under law, whether these are rock paintings or carvings, or scatterings of stone tools in a creek bed. It is an offence to disturb or remove artefacts found in the bush. While not all sites are specifically 'sacred sites', the land itself is sacred in the sense that Aboriginal spirituality embraces the land and everything above and below it. For Aboriginal people, the land is the source of their culture – the stories come from the land.

A note on the maps

Please note that it has not been possible to include all Aboriginal languages in those maps that cover whole states. Note also that the boundaries of the language areas are generally only approximate.

Further reading

There are numerous books on Australian languages, but most are written in technical language and are available only in university and major libraries. One readily available book is *Macquarie: Aboriginal Words* by Nick Thieberger and William McGregor (eds).

The languages in central Australia – or the Centre, as it's often called – are among the strongest surviving Aboriginal languages in the country, as their speakers have had a relatively short history of contact with non Aboriginal people. Despite this, the effects of non-Aboriginal settlement since it began in the 1870s have been dramatic. Before this time, it's thought that there were at least 38 main languages and dialects in the area. The establishment of pastoral properties, the Overland Telegraph Line, missions, reserves and later towns such as Alice Springs has meant that many language groups have moved, or have been moved, from their traditional country. Of the original 38 main languages and dialects, about 7 are now considered endangered, and 4 are considered extinct or nearly extinct.

The main surviving language groups in central Australia are the Arandic languages and dialects, dialects of the Western Desert language, dialects of Warlpiri, and Warumungu. These all belong to the Pama-Nyungan family (see page 140). The arid lands of central Australia can only support a limited number of people, and as a result, single language groups are spread over vast areas of land. The Western Desert language, for example, is one of the most widely spread indigenous languages in the world, extending from central Australia nearly to the Great Australian Bight and the Indian Ocean. Although languages in the Centre share a few common characteristics, they are for the most part very different from each other. Many people in this region are bilingual or multilingual, speaking one or more Aboriginal languages or dialects and English.

Central Australia

The names of languages and dialects used in central Australia are quite widely known. Often, they describe where the people who speak that language come from, or describe a feature of their language which distinguishes it from another language nearby, for example:

Ikngerre-ipenhe Arrernte   'eastern Arrernte'
Pitjantjatjara   'having the word *pitja*' (come)

Keeping languages strong

Apart from speaking their languages to their children and grandchildren, Aboriginal people are working hard in language centres, schools and media outlets to ensure that their languages survive. In Alice Springs, the Central Australian Aboriginal Media Association (CAAMA) produces films, television and documentaries in English and in local languages. Also in Alice Springs, Imparja Television broadcasts a number of hours of programs a day in Aboriginal languages. There are also a number of bands playing contemporary and more traditional Aboriginal music, including songs in Aboriginal languages, around the Centre. The CAAMA Shops (see details in Further Reading on page 158) stock CDs and some videos of local Aboriginal bands.

In Alice Springs, the Language and Culture Centre at the Institute for Aboriginal Development (IAD, www.iad.edu.au) runs language and cross-culture programs for Aboriginal and non-Aboriginal people from Alice Springs, as well as interstate and international visitors. The Institute also carries out research into central Australian languages, and produces dictionaries and other language-related publications. In Tennant Creek, Papulu Apparr-kari (the Barkly Region Aboriginal Language Centre, 17 Windley St, Tennant Creek, telephone 08 8962 3270) coordinates language and culture programs for its region.

There are several bilingual schools in the central Australian region, where Aboriginal children are taught in both their own language and in English. Most of these schools are in

Aboriginal communities, apart from Yipirinya School, an independent school in Alice Springs. Aboriginal people can study their own languages, or prepare for careers in interpreting and translating, language teaching or dictionary work by attending courses run by the IAD or the Batchelor Institute, an Aboriginal college based at Batchelor (south of Darwin) that has campuses in both Alice Springs and Tennant Creek.

Family relationships

Aboriginal people in central Australia think of themselves as related to all the people in their own language group, and often to people in other language groups as well. To regulate social behaviour, law and ceremony, and relationship to land, Aboriginal societies are typically divided into two or three sets of 'moieties' (a moiety is essentially a division of the society into two opposed and balanced halves). In many parts of Australia, the kinship and moiety groupings have been summarised in a neat and efficient way through what are commonly known as 'skin' groups or subsections.

The most common pattern is for there to be eight skin groups, often further divided into male and female groups (see the chart overleaf). A person is born into one of these skin groups and acquires the name of the skin group as well as a personal name. Various relatives are classed together in each skin group, and a person's position within this system determines their relationship and social and ceremonial obligations to all others in the language group. Kinship systems are too complex to describe fully here: if you want to learn more, IAD runs a one-day Aboriginal Cultural Awareness Program (ACAP) which provides some information in this area. See the IAD website for more details (www.iad.edu.au).

Central Australian Aboriginal skin names

	Western Desert Ngaany-atjarra	Pintupi/ Luritja	Warlpiri	Arrente & Anmatyerr
MOIETY 'Sun-side'				
Section				
Subsection male female	Yiparrka	Tjangala Nangala	Jangala Nangala	Angale
Subsection male female	Panaka	Tjupurrula Napurrula	Jupurrurla Napurrurla	Perrurle
Section	Tjarurru			
Subsection male female		Tjungurrayi Nungurrayi	Jungarrayi Nungurrayi	Kngwarraye
Subsection male female		Tjapanangka Njapanangka	Japanangka Njapanangka	Penangke
MOIETY 'Shade-side'				
Section				
Subsection male female	Milangka	Tjampitjinpa Nampitjinpa	Jampijinpa Nampijinpa	Ampetyane
Subsection male female	Karimarra	Tjakamarra Nakamarra	Jakamarra Nakamarra	Kemarre
Section	Purungu			
Subsection male female		Tjapangati Napangati	Japangardi Napangardi	Pengarte
Subsection male female		Tjapaltjarri Napaltjarri	Japaljarri Napaljarri	Peltharre

Travelling & staying on Aboriginal land

Many Aboriginal people in central Australia live in remote communities and out-stations, often on Aboriginal land. Most communities don't welcome visitors, except those who have a genuine reason to visit (for example, people who are connected with Aboriginal organisations or government departments, or who have been invited by someone in the community).

Some communities, however, have established tourism ventures, such as Hermannsburg and Wallace Rockhole (www.wallacerockholetours.com.au) southwest of Alice Springs. For information about tour operators on the Anangu Pitjantjatjara Lands in the northern part of South Australia, try contacting Desert Tracks (www.deserttracks.com.au).

You'll need a permit to visit or travel through all communities on Aboriginal land in central Australia, and as applications can sometimes take a few weeks to process, it's better to plan ahead. Application forms can be downloaded from the Central Land Council's website (www.clc.org.au).

If you're fortunate enough to have the opportunity to visit an Aboriginal community, don't leave the community on your own to go for a walk or do a bit of sightseeing – ask an Aboriginal person to go with you. They'll make sure that you don't stumble across any ceremonial camps or sacred areas that you shouldn't see. Also, make an effort to dress appropriately – make sure that your clothes are clean, and avoid revealing or tight clothing.

TAKING PHOTOGRAPHS

It's important to observe the usual courtesies in taking photographs of people – make sure that you ask for permission first, and if practical, offer to send copies of the photographs to them. It's also extremely important not to photograph sacred sites. In some popular tourist destinations, such as Uluru, there are signs at sacred sites requesting that you don't take photographs or use a video camera. Commercial photography and filming is prohibited in many areas. Contact the Central Land Council for details.

ALCOHOL

You are not allowed to carry alcohol into most central Australian Aboriginal communities. This rule is strictly enforced, and if you're caught, your vehicle may be confiscated and sold as a penalty. Most aren't returned, so don't take the risk!

Further reading

There are several places in Alice Springs that stock a range of books about Aboriginal culture and languages, if you want to learn more, and some that also sell paintings and artefacts. A few of these are owned by Aboriginal groups, including the Aboriginal Art and Culture Centre (www.aboriginalart.com.au) and IAD Press. IAD Press (www.iad.edu.au/press) is the publishing arm of the Institute for Aboriginal Development, and publishes materials produced by and for Aboriginal people about the languages and cultures of Central Australia. You can also contact CAAMA Shops Pty Ltd at 101 Todd St, Alice Springs, or visit the online shop at www.store.caama.com.au.

Arrernte languages

LANGUAGES & DIALECTS

The language name spelt 'Arrernte' in its own spelling system is perhaps better known outside central Australia as 'Aranda' or 'Arunta'. This language is part of a group of closely related languages and dialects known to linguists as the Arandic group (see map, page 160). The major language in this group has a number of dialects, including Central, Eastern, Western and Southern Arrernte, Eastern and Western Anmatyerr and Eastern and Western Alyawarr. There are two smaller languages in the group, not so closely related: Kaytetye to the north and Lower Arrernte, which is no longer spoken, to the south. The territory of the group comprises very roughly the southeastern quarter of the Northern Territory (of which

CENTRAL AUSTRALIA

158

a fairly big chunk, the Simpson Desert, is uninhabitable), and at one time also extended into South Australia north of Oodnadatta. Alice Springs is in Central Arrernte country. There are about 4500 speakers of languages of the group.

SOUNDS

The Arandic languages are believed to have had sound systems very much like their neighbouring languages, such as Warlpiri and Pitjantjatjara, at some time in the distant past, but they've changed drastically over the centuries. As an example, the word *wama* (snake) has become *apmwe*, *apme* and *mwang* in various dialects.

Vowels

The most common vowel in Arandic languages is written *e*, but its pronunciation depends very much on what sounds come immediately before and after it. Other vowels are *a* (similar to the *a* in 'father'), in some dialects; *i* (sounds like the vowels in 'air' or 'see', depending on what the next consonant is) and *u* (pronounced like the *u* in 'put' when it begins a word, or like the *o* in 'more' when it comes after the first consonant).

Consonants

The consonant system is quite complicated, with a number of sounds that exist in almost no other Australian language. One unfortunate result, from the point of view of writing, is that some sounds need to be written with two letters (such as *ly*, *nh*, *pm*, *rr*, *tn*) and some even need three letters (*kng*, *rtn*, *tnh*, *tny*).

WORD STRESS

Stress in Arandic languages is mostly on the vowel that follows the first consonant in a word, although in some dialects short words, such as *artwe* (man) and *iltye* (hand) are stressed on the initial vowel.

Arandic language group

NORTHERN TERRITORY

Tennant Creek

Camooweal

Mt Isa

Alyawarr

Kaytetye

Neutral Junction

Urandangi

Georgina

Yuendumu

Anmatyerr

Papunya

Mt Swan

Eastern Arrernte

Alice Springs

QUEENSLAND

Western Arrernte

Central Arrernte

Southern Arrernte

Simpson Desert

Finke

Finke

0 ————— 100 km
0 ————— 60 mi

SOUTH AUSTRALIA

▬ ▬ ▬ ▬ **Arandic language areas**

Based upon the IAD Language Centre map
*Current Distribution of Central
Australian Languages*

WA · NT · QLD · SA · NSW · VIC · TAS
AUSTRALIA

STRUCTURE

The Arandic languages belong to the suffixing category described on page 141 in the Indigenous languages chapter. The basic grammar of Central Arrernte is described in *A Learner's Guide to Eastern and Central Arrernte* by Jenny Green (IAD Press).

VOCABULARY

Some words that you may come across are:

aherre	red plains kangaroo
akatyerre	desert raisin
altyerre	Dreaming, the Law
alye	boomerang
arelhe	Aboriginal person
arlewatyerre	sand goanna
atneme	woman's digging stick
atyunpe	perentie (large lizard)
inernte	bean tree
irrtyarte	spear
kere	meat or animal used for food
kwatye	water
lhentere	non-Aboriginal person
merne	food, especially vegetable foods and bread
ngkwarle	sweet things
ntyarlke	elephant grub
pmerlpe	quandong (edible fruit)
rapite	rabbit
tyape	edible grubs
tyerrtye	Aboriginal person
untyeye	corkwood
urtne	coolamon (a shallow wooden dish)
utyerrke	bush fig
warlpele	non-Aboriginal person
yeperenye	caterpillar that lives on the tar vine
yerrampe	honey ant

ARRERNTE PLACE NAMES

The Arrernte name for the Alice Springs area is *Mparntwe*, while Heavitree Gap is *Ntaripe*. The MacDonnell Ranges as a whole are called *Tyurretye* (sometimes spelt *Choritja*). Prominent Central Australian mountains include: *Rwetyepme* (Mt Sonder), *Urlatherrke* (Mt Zeil) and *Alhekulyele* (Mt Gillen).

Other well-known scenic spots in Arrernte country, in the Eastern MacDonnell Ranges, include:

Anthwerrke	Emily Gap
Ilwentye	Ndhala Gorge
Inteyarrkwe	Ross River
Kepalye	Jessie Gap

And in the Western MacDonnell Ranges:

Angkele	Standley Chasm
Kwartetweme	Ormiston Gorge
Twipethe	Ellery Creek Big Hole
Urrengetyirrpe	Simpsons Gap
Yaperlpe	Glen Helen Gorge

Arrernte place names fall into two groups. One type is when the name describes the place; for example, the Finke River is *Lherepirnte* (anglicised as Larapinta). This is composed of *lhere* (river) and *pirnte* (salt), although there's some doubt about this, as *pirnte* means 'spring (of water)' in some dialects. Likewise, the name of the town Finke is *Aperturl* (usually spelt 'Aputula'), which translates as 'hill-forehead' and refers to a nearby hill.

The second type of name is taken from the Dreaming (Aboriginal creation history) of the area. For example, an area in Alice Springs is called *Ntyarlkarletyaneme* (the place where the elephant grub crosses over). *Ntyarlke* (the elephant grub) is one of the ancestral caterpillar beings which created much of the landscape around Alice Springs, as well as being a kind of caterpillar still found in the area. Some hills in the area covered by the name are parts of the body of these ancestral beings (have a look at the signs at the golf course!). Further east, in the MacDonnell Ranges, the name for Emily Gap, *Anthwerrke*, means 'small intestine' and refers to the guts of the caterpillar.

FURTHER READING

A Town Like Mparntwe by David Brooks (IAD Press) gives readers an insight into the traditional history of Mparntwe (Alice Springs), and offers a fascinating travelogue of the region. *Bush Foods: Arrernte Foods of Central Australia* by Margaret Kemarre Turner (IAD Press) takes a comprehensive look at traditional bush foods in Mparntwe and surrounding areas.

Western Desert language

LANGUAGES & DIALECTS

The Western Desert language spreads over a vast area of desert country (see the map on the following page). Dialects of Western Desert include Pitjantjatjara, Yankunytjatjara, Ngaanyatjarra, Ngaatjatjarra, Pintupi, Papunya Luritja, Luritja, Matutjara, Kukatja, Antikirinya, Mantjiltjara and Kartutjara.

In all, it's estimated that there are between 4000 and 5000 speakers of Western Desert dialects, with Pitjantjatjara being one of the better known varieties. Most of the Pitjantjatjara and Yankunytjatjara people live on the Anangu Pitjantjatjara freehold lands in the northwest of South Australia, or just over the borders in Western Australia and the Northern Territory.

Visitors to central Australia are likely to meet speakers of Pitjantjatjara and Yankunytjatjara at Uluru (Ayers Rock) and Kata Tjuta (the Olgas), and Pitjantjatjara and Luritja speakers at Watarrka (Kings Canyon).

Western Desert language group

Lajamanu

WESTERN AUSTRALIA

Ord

Victoria

Fitzroy

Billiluna

Balgo

Kukatja

NORTHERN TERRITORY

0 — 200 km
0 — 120 mi

Gibson Desert

Lake Mackay

Pintupi

Kintore

Papunya Luritja

Papunya

Macdonnell Ranges

Watarrka (Kings Canyon)

Luritja

Alice Springs

Docker River

Lake Amadeus

Ngaatjatjarra

Uluru

Simpson Desert

Ngaanyatjarra

Warburton

Pitjantjatjara

SOUTH AUSTRALIA

Oodnadatta

Great Victoria Desert

Yankunytjatjara

Coober Pedy

Western Desert language areas

Based upon the IAD Language Centre map
Current Distribution of Central Australian Languages

NT
WA   QLD
        SA   NSW
AUSTRALIA VIC
            TAS

ULURU & KATA TJUTA

Both of these landmarks are on the border between Pitjantjatjara and Yankunytjatjara country. The name 'Uluru' is thought by some people to be derived from *ulerenye*, an Arrernte word for 'stranger'. *Kata Tjuta* translates into English as 'heads' or 'many heads'. There are signs around the base of Uluru and at Kata Tjuta in Pitjantjatjara, with English translations. An excellent way to learn more about the language and culture is to take a self-guided walk using the brochures available from the Uluru–Kata Tjuta Cultural Centre, or book a guided tour with Anangu Tours (www.anangutours.com.au).

Pitjantjatjara and Yankunytjatjara people call tourists *minga tjuta* (ants). If you stand at the base of Uluru, and watch people climbing, you'll understand why. Although it's not widely advertised, the traditional owners of Uluru would prefer that you didn't climb the rock. There's a sign explaining this at the base of the climb. Apart from the damage being caused to sacred sites, the traditional owners are worried about the number of people who have been killed or injured during the climb.

VOCABULARY

Some words that you may come across are:

anangu	Aboriginal person
anumara	edible caterpillar
Ili	bush fig
ininti	bean tree
kali	boomerang
kampurarpa	desert raisin
kapi	water
katji/kulata	spear
kuka	meat or animal used for food
kurku	honeydew on mulga (an acacia shrub)
mai	food, especially vegetable foods and bread

maku	edible grubs, especially witchetty grubs (a grub that lives in the roots of the witchetty bush)
malu	red plains kangaroo
ngintaka	perentie (large lizard)
piranpa	non-Aboriginal person
piti	coolamon (wooden bowl used to carry water)
rapita	rabbit
tinka	sand goanna
tjala	honey ant
tjukurpa	Dreaming, the Law
walypala	non-Aboriginal person
wama	sweet things (nowadays also used to refer to alcohol)
wana	women's digging stick
wayanu	quandong (edible fruit)
witjinti	corkwood

WATARRKA

Watarrka (Kings Canyon) is in Luritja country, and takes its name from a type of acacia known as the umbrella bush (*Acacia ligulata*) that grows in the valley below the canyon. There are signs around the canyon walk in Pitjantjatjara, with English translations.

FURTHER READING

If you want to learn more, try *Wangka Wiru: A handbook for the Pitjantjatjara language learner*, by Paul Eckert and Joyce Hudson (University of South Australia). Also, IAD Press has various dictionaries to languages in this region, including Ngaanyatjarra and Ngaatjatjara, Pintupi/Luritja and Pitjantjatjara/Yankunytjatjara, and publishes *A Learners' Guide to Pintupi/Luritja* and *A Learners' Guide to Pitjantjatjara/ Yankunytjatjara*.

Warlpiri

LANGUAGES & DIALECTS

Warlpiri is part of the Ngarrkic language group (see the map on page 168). There are thought to be at least 3000 Warlpiri speakers, most of whom speak Warlpiri as their first language. They live in a number of quite large communities around the edge of traditional Warlpiri country: Yurntumu (Yuendumu), Lajamanu (which used to be called Hooker Creek, and is actually on Kurindji country), Wirliyajarrayi (Willowra) and Nyirrpi (which is strictly speaking a Pintupi community). But many Warlpiri spend at least part of the year in the numerous out-stations (small communities) in Warlpiri country, the heart of which is the Tanami Desert (named by Europeans after Janami rockhole, near the junction of the Tanami road and the Lajamanu road). There are also substantial Warlpiri populations in other communities around traditional Warlpiri country, especially on Kaytetye country in Alekarenge (a Kaytetye name referring to Dog Dreaming, also written 'Ali Curung' and which used to be called Warrabri), and in towns such as Alice Springs on Arrernte country, Tennant Creek on Warumungu country, and Katherine on Jawoyn country.

Warlpiri is still a very vigorous language, and though it's being lost by Warlpiri children in some communities that lie outside the traditional country (usually to Aboriginal English or an Aboriginal creole), it's nonetheless spreading well outside its traditional country, and is also spoken by 1000 or more people as a second language over a very large area extending as far north as Darwin, west to Fitzroy Crossing in Western Australia, east to Tennant Creek and other Barkly Tableland communities, and south to Alice Springs and the northern Western Desert communities.

There are five major dialects of Warlpiri: Warrmarla or Ngardilypa to the west, Warnayaka to the north, Ngaliya to the south, Yarlpiri or Warlpiri in the Lander River area in the heart of Warlpiri country, and Wakirti Warlpiri in the Hansen River area to the east. The main differences are in vocabulary and pronunciation, reflecting the influences of neighbouring

Ngarrkic language group

Ord

WESTERN
AUSTRALIA

NORTHERN
TERRITORY

○ *Lajamanu*

○ Tennant
Creek

○ *Tanami*

Tanami Desert

○ *Balgo*

Warlpiri

*Lake
Mackay*

○ *Yuendumu*

Hann Range

Gibson Desert

Papunya ○

○ *Alice Springs*

| 0 | | 100 km |
| 0 | | 60 mi |

■ **Ngarrkic language area**

Language locations approximate only.

Based upon the IAD Language Centre map
*Current Distribution of Central
Australian Languages*

WA — NT — QLD
SA — NSW
AUSTRALIA — VIC
TAS

languages, but they are mutually comprehensible. Though the Warlpiri will sometimes emphasise the dialect differences, they generally consider themselves to be one people with one language, Warlpiri.

Warlpiri has a spelling system which has been in use since 1974, mainly in the context of bilingual education programs in the schools of the main Warlpiri communities. Nowadays, most young to middle-aged Warlpiri can read and write their language.

VOCABULARY

Some words that you may come across are:

jukurrpa	Dreaming, the Law
jurlarda	bush honey
kardiya	non-Aboriginal person
karli	boomerang
kuyu	meat or animal used for food
mangarriyi	food, especially vegetable foods and bread
marlu	red plains kangaroo
miyi	food, especially vegetable foods and bread
ngapa	water
ngarlkirdi	witchetty grub
ngayaki	bush tomato
ngurlu	grain; seeds
pama	delicacy (nowadays also used to refer to alcohol)
parraja	coolamon, dish used to separate grains and chaff and carry babies and food
wardapi	sand goanna
yankirri	emu
yapa	Aboriginal person
yarla	bush potato

FURTHER READING

IAD Press publishes Warlpiri learning materials, including *A Learner's Guide to Warlpiri* by Mary Laughren and Robert Hoogenraad.

ABORIGINAL ENGLISH

Aboriginal people often speak a distinctive form of English. In southeastern Australia this differs from mainstream English in that there are old-fashioned English words like *plant* 'to hide' and *gammon* 'to pretend' or 'to deceive', plus some Aboriginal words such as *binjy* 'stomach' and *bogey* 'to bathe'. These are words from the Sydney area that have been widely disseminated. It's also common to find words such as *kuna* 'faeces' and *marra* 'hand' which are widespread in Aboriginal languages, plus some words from local languages.

In the north of Australia, Aboriginal English exhibits the same features as in the south plus various degrees of similarity to Kriol (see page 146). Aboriginal people are likely to use *he* and *fella* for females as well as males, for instance, or use *mother* for their mother's sister as well as their real mother. Past tense is rendered by *bin*, and *longa* or *alonga* substitutes for a variety of English prepositions, so we find *That one bin fightin' alonga nother fella* for 'That one was fighting with another person.' That's clear enough, but the use of *meself* as a general reflexive pronoun is confusing. *Them blackfellas bin fightin meself* sounds as if it means 'Those Aborigines were fighting me', but in fact it means 'Those Aborigines were fighting one another.'

Aboriginal English often includes English words used with ranges of meaning that match those of words from Aboriginal languages. *Shame*, for instance, covers modesty as well as shame, and the types of breach of good conduct that are grounds for shame are wider than in European culture. Another example is the expression *no more*, which can correspond to 'no more' in English or can simply mean 'no' or 'not'.

The fact that some Aboriginal people speak English with an 'Aboriginal accent' – ie with phonetic features characteristic of their native language – can also be a source of confusion. There are reports of people hearing *spinifex* as 'penny fag', and *tongue* as 'dung', or failing to understand a word or two altogether. This is no different, of course, to any other non-native speaker of English who has an accent.

In the 'Top End', the northern half of the Northern Territory, there are a large number of languages of the prefixing type, though there is also an enclave of Pama-Nyungan languages in northeast Arnhem Land. (See the Indigenous languages chapter, page 140, for more information.)

Land rights

Membership in a particular language is of great social and cultural significance, and land, language and people are inextricably bound together in Aboriginal culture. Traditionally, languages belong to tracts of country (often having been put in their places by Dreamtime creator figures); therefore Aboriginal people belong to their country and to their languages. Ownership of particular country and its associated language(s) is inherited through either or both parents, depending on the area.

Much of the northeast of the Northern Territory is part of Arnhem Land, a reserve established in 1933 and granted Aboriginal title under the *Aboriginal Land Rights Act* (NT) of 1976. In recent years, many Aboriginal language groups have been able to claim back (part of) their traditional lands through this Act. However, not all Aboriginal groups have been able to regain possession of their land, due to the provisions in the legislation about the kind of land that can be claimed and who can be recognised as traditional owners.

It was in part the regaining of the ownership of and access to traditional lands which made the homeland centres movement possible. 'Homeland centre' is the term commonly used in the northeast region for what in other areas are called 'out-stations' – small communities in a group's traditional country. The movement began in the 1970s and saw family groups opting to move out of larger communities to their traditional lands to start homeland centres with populations of 15 to 100.

It should be noted that access to Aboriginal land and communities is restricted and monitored by a system of permits. People who want to visit must apply in advance to the relevant land council or community council – the Northern Land Council for most of the Top End, Anindilyakwa Land Council for Groote Eylandt and Central Land Council for some of the more southerly areas.

Historical influences

MAKASSANS

During at least the last two centuries before European invasion, Aboriginal peoples of the north coast of Australia had regular interaction with people from further north. These people were known as 'Makassans' after the Indonesian city Makassar (Ujung Pandang), though many of the visitors came from other areas, and came south every year for *trepang* (sea cucumbers). The legacy of their visits can be seen in material items, family ties, language and ceremony. When Europeans first attempted to create settlements on the north coast near Darwin in the 1800s, they recorded that Aboriginal people addressed them using a Malay pidgin which had presumably been acquired through their long-term contact with Makassans or other seafaring peoples from the archipelago to the north. Words from Makassan are found in many northern Aboriginal languages. Examples from the Yolŋu languages include:

bathala	big, important (Makassan: *bàttala* 'heavy; big; onerous')
detuŋ	buffalo – pronounced 'diitung' (Makassan: *tèdong* 'water buffalo')
rrupiya	money (Makassan: *rupiya* 'money')

The Makassan voyages ceased in 1906 when they were banned by the Australian government. In recent times, however, contact has been re-established. People from Yolŋu communities have visited Makassar and met relatives there. In 1988, a *prau* (canoe-like sailing boat) re-enacted the voyages of old, bringing relatives and others from Makassar to old hunting grounds and families in East Arnhem Land.

EUROPEAN INVASION

The history of the European invasion and takeover of the Top End is important to the understanding of the present linguistic situation. In areas where Europeans settled early and in large numbers, such as around the Darwin region and southwards along the Stuart Highway, traditional languages are no longer spoken.

In the drier open savanna country, cattle stations were set up using the labour of Aboriginal people. Aboriginal station 'employees' – their wage and living conditions often amounted to little better than slavery – had to be able to communicate in English. It's difficult to generalise about the effect that cattle stations had on Top End language groups. Where Aboriginal 'employees' were predominantly from the same language group, as at Wave Hill Station (Gurindji language group) and Humbert River Station (Ngarinyman language group), it was possible for people to continue speaking their traditional language in some situations, such as in the camp or out bush. The seasonal nature of the work – there was little or no work available during the Wet – also meant that Aboriginal 'employees' relied upon their traditional knowledge to survive.

Around the Top End coastline missions were established; their effect on Aboriginal language groups depended a great deal on the individual institution and on the circumstances of the area. In some instances, missionaries forbade the use of traditional languages, whereas in others Europeans working with a mission were expected to learn the traditional languages. At some missions, the so-called dormitory system was enforced, whereby children were housed separately from their parents in dormitories. This was particularly disruptive to the transmission of traditional languages.

Current language situation

The Top End languages provide examples of all the possible post-colonial fates of indigenous languages – from no speakers at all to full use in all everyday activities.

In areas with large, long-term European settlement like Darwin and Katherine, the traditional languages are no longer spoken. Any traditional languages spoken by Aboriginal people in these places are from other areas. In Darwin, this could be Tiwi from Bathurst or Melville Islands or one of the Yolŋu languages from East Arnhem Land, among many other possibilities. In Katherine, visitors might hear Warlpiri from the desert country in the far southwest of the region.

Traditional Aboriginal languages are still spoken in more isolated areas where contact with non-Aboriginal people has been most recent. Areas where traditional languages are still fully spoken include the Daly River region southwest of Darwin, Bathurst and Melville Islands to the north of Darwin, the Arnhem Land Reserve to the east, Groote Eylandt in the Gulf of Carpentaria and the desert region at the southwestern edge of the Top End.

In many areas with a lot of non-Aboriginal visitors, such as Kakadu National Park, Litchfield or Nitmiluk (Katherine Gorge), only older members of the Aboriginal community know their ancestral languages fluently. Younger people may well understand and use some traditional language but they mostly speak Kriol, a dialect of Aboriginal English or another traditional language.

LANGUAGE SHIFT

In communities where traditional languages continue to be used, some languages are growing in numbers of speakers while others are declining. This is due to language shifts from one traditional language to another, in part because of changing demographic patterns. Formerly, small numbers of people lived in isolated clan groups and this isolation fostered the maintenance of many distinct language varieties. These days, even in relatively isolated areas, people tend to live for at least some of the year in large regional communities populated by members of different language groups. In such multilingual communities there's a trend for one language to emerge as a lingua franca.

At Maningrida community, for example, on the coast of central Arnhem Land, there are members of at least eight different language groups, and two of the local languages are gradually emerging as lingua francas: one used by people who affiliate with the 'west side' (Kunwinjku and its eastern dialects), the other used by people who affiliate with the 'east side' (Burarra). Children growing up at Maningrida tend to learn one of these emergent lingua francas because these are the languages that they hear spoken around them most often and which enable them to communicate with the largest number of people. There's widespread concern about the languages being passed over in favour of a lingua franca.

Katherine Region

Aboriginal people nowadays use the terms 'sun-go-down' (or 'sunset') to refer to the people, lands and languages in the western Katherine Region (approximately west of the Stuart Highway) and 'sunrise' to refer to those in the east of the region. This division reflects the perceived differences in the nature of the languages, in the groups they're affiliated with, in traditional culture, in climate and country and even in art styles. (Abstract 'dot paintings' are typical of the western Katherine Region, whereas figures and lined artwork typify the east side.)

KATHERINE

The township of Katherine is the administrative centre of the region and it's possible to find members of all the language groups of the Katherine Region there as well as many others from even further afield. Of the three Aboriginal languages traditionally spoken in and around Katherine, Dagoman is no longer spoken and Jawoyn is spoken only by some older people. Wardaman is slightly 'stronger' in that it's been transmitted to some younger people who speak or understand it. The Aboriginal language that visitors to Katherine will definitely hear is Kriol. With the exception of Lajamanu in the far southwest, Aboriginal communities have a variety of Kriol as a first or main language.

SUN-GO-DOWN (WESTERN REGION)

The country is drier here than elsewhere in the Top End. The Victoria River is the only major river system in the entire region. There are four main areas of Aboriginal population, from south to north: Lajamanu; Daguragu and Kalkaringi; Pigeon Hole, Yarralin and Lingara; and communities in the environs of Timber Creek.

Lajamanu is now a Warlpiri-speaking community, because white authorities moved large numbers of Warlpiri people (see page 167) away from their traditional homelands farther south and onto lands traditionally owned by Kartangarrurru and Gurindji people. At Lajamanu, children are still acquiring Warlpiri as their first language and the community has a bilingual program operating at the school.

At Kalkaringi (the old government settlement of Wave Hill) and Daguragu (the old strike camp of Wattie Creek), however, Gurindji is still spoken, although the main language of the children and young adults is a variety of Kriol that is influenced by Gurindji. Even so, children and young people mostly have a thorough understanding of Gurindji as well. The Gurindji people are famous for the Wave Hill Strike of 1966, which fought back at the shocking wage and living conditions endured by Aboriginal people working on cattle stations at that time and which eventuated in a fight for land rights.

To the east of Gurindji is Mudburra, which is spoken across as far as Elliott. To the west are Nyininy and Malngin, language varieties that are closely related to Gurindji.

Bilinarra country lies to the north of Gurindji around the Pigeon Hole and Yarralin communities. However, Ngarinyman is the main traditional language represented at Yarralin and it's spoken over a large area to the northwest as far as Kununurra and northwards to communities around Timber Creek.

Speakers of four main language groups have settled in communities in and around Timber Creek: Ngarinyman, Ngaliwurru, Nungali and Jaminjung. Traditional country for the Ngaliwurru includes the spectacular Stokes Ranges. Nungali appears to be a threatened language with very few remaining speakers. Jaminjung is spoken to the west as far as Kununurra and to the north in some Daly Region communities.

To the west of these languages, two further language groups occupy country in the Northern Territory: the Miriwoong and the Gajirrang (also known as Gajirrabeng and Gajirrawoong), although members of these language groups mostly reside in Kununurra and nearby communities in Western Australia today.

To the southwest of Katherine lies the traditional country of the Wardaman people. Most Wardaman people live in and around the town of Katherine nowadays. However, the Wardaman Association owns and operates Innesvale Station and there are also a number of small family out-stations on Wardaman country. Wardaman was mutually intelligible with the traditional languages spoken near Katherine (Dagoman) and Mataranka (Yangman). However, unlike Dagoman and Yangman, which are no longer spoken, Wardaman is still spoken and/or understood by some younger people today.

SUNRISE (EASTERN REGION)

The 'sunrise' (eastern) side of the Katherine Region extends from the Stuart Highway across to the 'saltwater country' bordering the Gulf of Carpentaria. From south to north it reaches from the 'dry country' north of the Barkly Tableland, through the 'freshwater country' associated with the Roper and Katherine River systems and their tributaries, to the

Aboriginal languages of the Katherine Region

JOSEPH BONAPARTE GULF

Daly

Mayali

Pine Creek

Wagiman

Jawoyn

Dagoman

Barunga

Katherine

Fitzmaurice

Jaminjung

Wardaman

Yangman

Mataranka

Gajirrang

Miriwoong

Nungali

Timber Creek

Ngaliwurru

Karangpurru

NORTHERN TERRITORY

Lake Argyle

Amanbidji

Ngarinyman

Yarralin

Victoria

Top Springs

Pigeon Hole

WESTERN AUSTRALIA

Bilinarra

Mudburra

Malngin

Kalkaringi

Gurindji

Kartangurru

Nyininy

Lajamanu

Warlpiri

■ **Languages of the Katherine Region**
Language locations approximate only.

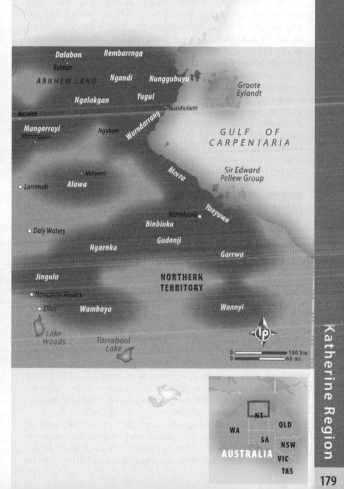

'stone country' of the Arnhem Land escarpment. The major centres of Aboriginal population include Borroloola on the McArthur River, Ngukurr on the Roper River, Minyerri (formerly Hodgson Downs), Jilkminggan at the headwaters of the Roper and the communities of Barunga, Beswick and Bulman on the Central Arnhem Highway.

Borroloola is situated on the traditional country of the Yanyuwa, although members of surrounding language groups such as Garrwa, Gudanyji and Marra all live in and around Borroloola nowadays. An interesting feature of Yanyuwa is that women's speech is structurally different to the variety spoken by men. The differences include a separate system of prefixes used when a woman is talking about a man – she must use the prefix *ny(a)-* on the noun and any adjectives referring to him:

'You disobedient boy!'	
woman speaking:	man speaking:
yenda ny-ardu nya-mordo (lit: you boy deaf)	*yenda ardu mordo* (lit: you boy deaf)

To the north of Borroloola, on the Roper River, is the community of Ngukurr and several smaller communities and outstations. The linguistic situation here is highly complex. People affiliated with numerous language groups including Ngalakgan, Warndarrang (also spelt 'Warndarraŋ'), Yugul, Marra, Ngandi, Alawa, Nunggubuyu, Ritharrŋu and Rembarrnga now live at Ngukurr. Of these languages, Warndarrang and Yugul are no longer spoken, Ngandi and Ngalakgan have very few remaining speakers and Alawa and Marra are spoken fully only by some older people. Rembarrnga and Ritharrŋu probably have relatively greater numbers of speakers in more remote communities.

Minyerri and Jilkminggan, communities further east in the Roper Valley, are on Alawa and Mangarrayi country respectively. The writings of Jeannie Gunn, such as *We of the Never-Never*, were based on her experiences of Elsey Station in Mangarrayi country. Mangarrayi, like Alawa and Marra mentioned above, is only spoken fully by some older people.

The Barunga, Beswick and Bulman communities are located in Central Arnhem Land to the north of the Roper Valley on the Central Arnhem Highway. Barunga and Beswick were formerly part of Bamyili, a government reserve. The traditional owners for this country are Jawoyn. The popular tourist destinations Nitmiluk (Katherine Falls) and Leliny (Edith Falls) are also on Jawoyn country. However, speakers from other language groups – including Mayali, Dalabon and Rembarrnga – form a large proportion of the population at Barunga and Beswick. At Bulman, the major language groups represented are Dalabon and Rembarrnga, which are spoken fully by some older adults – younger adults tend to be able to understand their traditional languages but don't usually speak them fully.

Kriol

Kriol is a new Aboriginal language that has upwards of 20,000 speakers throughout most of the Katherine Region and the neighbouring Kimberley Region in Western Australia. The name 'Kriol' has been applied to it relatively recently and has not yet gained widespread currency among all of its speakers.

As the name suggests, Kriol is a creole language – this means that it's a kind of 'emergency language' which has a specific origin. Kriol first arose early in the 20th century when surviving members of many decimated language groups fled to the Roper River Mission to escape the brutal killings being carried out by cattle station companies in the area at that time. Many of the adults who came to the Roper River Mission were multilingual, but they were certainly not multilingual in exactly the same languages. Moreover, their children had not yet developed full competence in as many languages. In this situation, the only form of language available for communication among everybody – including the English-speaking missionaries – was a pidgin that had entered the Northern Territory a few decades previously with the cattle trade and had become fairly widespread. Children at the mission heard more of this pidgin than of any other language, not least because the missionaries housed them in dormitories away from their elders. The children acquired the pidgin as their first language and, in doing so, created a full language which was able to meet all their communicative needs.

Due to its origins, Kriol has elements in common with traditional Aboriginal languages, with English and with other creole languages. As 'new' languages, creole languages tend to have fewer of the irregularities that occur in older languages and they also tend to convey most kinds of linguistic meaning with separate words. So whereas English can use the ending *-ed* to indicate past time, Kriol always uses a separate word, *bin*, to indicate an action that happened in the past. For example, *bin luk* means 'looked'.

Traditional Aboriginal languages have played a very important part in shaping Kriol's sound system, and in some of its structural features, as well as providing many vocabulary items and meanings. Just like most traditional Aboriginal languages, Kriol doesn't distinguish between pairs of sounds like *b/p*, *d/t*, *g/k*, *f/v* or *s/z*, nor does it use *sh*.

SOUNDS

All the letters used to represent Kriol sounds can be pronounced as in English, except for:

- *a* as in 'father'
- *e* as in 'bed'
- *u* as in 'put'
- *i* (mostly) as in 'week', or (sometimes) as in 'tin'
- *o* (mostly) as in 'port', or (sometimes) as in 'nod'
- *ai* as in 'aisle'
- *ei* as in 'hay'
- *oi* as in 'noise'
- *g* as in 'go' (never as in 'George')
- *th* as in 'this' (never as in 'thin')
- *rr* sounds a bit like the rolled *r* in Scottish English, Spanish and Italian

VOCABULARY

Kriol speakers use large numbers of words from their traditional languages, especially in areas of traditional knowledge like place names, traditional items like boomerangs and coolamons, names for local flora and fauna, and for personal information like Aboriginal personal names, relationship terms and body parts. Kriol speakers who live in different areas draw on different traditional Aboriginal languages for this kind of vocabulary, so Kriol can vary a great deal from place to place.

Kriol also uses many words that are more closely aligned with meanings represented in traditional Aboriginal languages – even if the actual 'shape' of the word is derived from English. So if a Kriol speaker talks about his or her *mami* (mother), don't be tricked into thinking the Kriol word has the same meaning as its English counterpart. *Mami* refers to traditional Aboriginal kinship concepts – although it can mean someone's biological mother, it can also refer to that woman's sisters, to her husband's brothers' wives, and to the countless women who carry the same skin name as any of these people (see page 155 for more about skin names).

STRUCTURE

In some ways Kriol also resembles traditional Aboriginal languages structurally. For instance, many traditional Aboriginal languages and Kriol don't have a class of separate adjectives.

Nouns

Kriol uses a variety of words preceding nouns to indicate plurals. However, there's a fair amount of leeway in Kriol as to whether plurals are marked or not – sometimes it's already obvious from the context if the reference is plural.

ola	*plural marker*
ola biliken	(the) billycans
ola kenggurru	(the) kangaroos

If Kriol speakers are referring to just two of something (dual number), they have to mark this with **dubala** (sometimes **tubala**).

>**dubala/tubala** *dual marker*
>**dubala gel**   (the) two girls

Verbs

Kriol indicates past time with the marker **bin** before a verb, as mentioned on page 182. For example:

>**Minbala bin wok gada ola biliken.**
>The two of us walked with the billycans.

This joins with the form **im** (he/she/it) to make **imin**:

>**imin laithad la melabat**
>he said to all of us
>(lit: he-was like-that to all-of-us)

Once a story has been established in the past, Kriol doesn't necessarily mark every instance of a verb with **bin**.

Future time (and also necessity) are expressed with the marker **gada** (or **garra**) before a verb. This marker sounds the same as some of the forms of the word **gada** meaning 'with', so it can be a little confusing:

>**Yumob gada gu gada yumob matha.**
>You lot *will* go <u>with</u> your mother.
>You lot *have to* go <u>with</u> your mother.

Kriol has some interesting tools for indicating 'a lot of' an action or an event. These can be used independently or they can be combined to achieve various nuances. If something would occur regularly or habitually, Kriol uses the marker **oldei** meaning 'usually', 'habitually', 'always', 'would' etc (often shortened to **ala**). **Oldei** was originally derived from the English expression 'all day', but obviously doesn't have much in common with it now.

Melabat bin oldei gu fishing en hanting.
> We all would go fishing and hunting.
> We all usually went fishing and hunting.

If there's a lot of something happening – for example, when a lot of people are involved, or there's a repeated series of events – Kriol often doubles up the verb:

Mela bin gula-gula gija olawei.
> We were telling off each other all the way.

If something happens for an uninterrupted time span (especially when this is subsequently interrupted or ended), Kriol speakers will often lengthen or stretch out a word as they say it. The pitch of the lengthened word is markedly higher than the surrounding words, so it sounds almost like singing.

Minbala bin oldei wok-w-o-o-o-k.
> The two of us would keep on walking.

Kriol doesn't have any one item that's directly equivalent to the English verb 'to be'. To indicate the meaning 'to be in a place or state', the Kriol verb ***jidan*** (sometimes also ***sidun***) 'stay', 'stop', 'sit' may be used:

jidan kwait
> stay quiet, be quiet

Mela ol jidan la kemp.
> We all stop in the camp.
> We are all in the camp.

However, where the orientation of something is important, such as vertical versus horizontal, or is inherent in its nature (for example, trees 'stand' in Kriol), Kriol always prefers the use of more specific verbs, like ***jendap*** (stand, be vertical).

To say 'something is something' (ie 'X is Y'), Kriol just places the items together with no intervening element:

Thad trubala.
> That is true.

Kriol

Kriol remains primarily a spoken language, used for everyday communication in all-Aboriginal contexts. Various bands from the Katherine Region have used Kriol in their songs. However, it's also used as a language of instruction and in initial literacy work in the bilingual school program at Barunga Community where many Kriol texts for children have been produced. There's also a Kriol Bible translation and a Kriol–English dictionary.

Darwin & the nearby coast

Larrikiya is the language of the traditional owners of Darwin (see the map on page 190). Today it's spoken only by a few elderly people. For other languages of the Darwin region, such as Wuna and Limilngan, the situation is the same. You'll certainly hear many different Aboriginal languages spoken on the streets of Darwin, but none of them will be Larrikiya. The languages you'll hear will be indigenous to other areas, spoken by people who are immigrants or visitors to town. Members of the Larrikiya community are currently working to record and revive their ancestral language. Larrikiya words are used in songs written and performed by the Darwin group, the Mills Sisters.

Tiwi continues to be spoken on Bathurst and Melville Islands immediately to the north of Darwin. (Bathurst Island is a popular tourist destination and texts produced in Tiwi language are available for purchase by visitors.) Traditional Tiwi is a highly complex language, although under the influence of English a simpler variety has arisen with fewer affixes and fewer of those words that correspond to whole sentences in English (an example was quoted on page 146).

Along the coast to the east of Darwin are several groups of languages. Very little is known about any of the languages spoken between Darwin and Kakadu. Only very old people still speak the languages of Kakadu and the Gurig Peninsula – most younger people now speak one of the closely related dialects Mayali and Kunwinjku. Mawng, the traditional language of Goulburn Island, and Iwaja, the language of the eastern part of the Cobourg Peninsula, are still spoken in the area. Kunbarlang is a coastal relative of Kunwinjku and was spoken west of the Liverpool River; however, most young Barlang people now speak Kunwinjku. A small language group comprising distant relatives of the Kunwinjkuan language family is spoken in the area around Maningrida in central coastal Arnhem Land, between the Liverpool and Blyth Rivers. The languages in this group are Ndjébbana (also called Kunibidji), Nakkara, Burarra, Gunnartpa and Gurrgoni.

Northern central region

Most of the languages spoken in the interior part of the Top End are related to one another as members of the Kunwinjkuan family. Languages in this family include Warray, Jawoyn, Bininj Kunwok (with dialects including Mayali, Kunwinjku, Kuninjku and Kune), Kunbarlang, Rembarrnga, Dalabon (also called Dangbon and Ngalkbon), Ngalakgan, Ngandi and Ngunggubuyu. Kunwinjkuan languages are spoken around the Arnhem Land Escarpment.

Warray is spoken by a few elderly people in the Pine Creek area. Jawoyn is spoken by some older people in Katherine, Pine Creek, Barunga and Beswick, around the southwestern edge of the escarpment. Bininj Kunwok – literally, 'people's language' – is a series of dialects spoken in a chain around the western and northern rim of the escarpment. Mayali is in the west, Kunwinjku in the northwest (Gunbalanya area), Kuninjku in the Liverpool River area and Kune on the eastern rim of the escarpment.

Dalabon (also known as Dangbon and Ngalkbon), and Rembarrnga are traditionally spoken around the eastern edge of the escarpment. Dalabon and Rembarrnga are today spoken on the northern rim of the escarpment at homeland centres such as Korlobidahda, Buluh Karduru and Malnjangarnak, and also at communities situated south of the escarpment such as Bulman, Beswick and Barunga. Both the Ngalakgan and Ngandi languages, once spoken to the southeast toward the Roper River region, are today spoken by just a few elderly people.

Maningrida is an important regional centre and is situated in a transitional area between east and west Arnhem Land. There are significant cultural differences between Arnhem Landers who affiliate with the 'west side' and those who affiliate with the 'east side'. Burarra people affiliate with the east side and the Burarra language has been used in albums recorded by the Maningrida Sunrize Band. A variety of Bininj Kunwok is the language of the inhabitants of Maningrida who are affiliated with the west side.

STRUCTURE

Kunwinjkuan languages have complex verbs with pronouns prefixed to the verb and object nouns incorporated into the verb. For example, in Kunwinjku, *Birri-gug-nang* is 'They saw the body' with *birri* 'they', *gug* 'body' and *nang* 'saw'.

Most Kunwinjkuan languages have a system of grammatical gender or noun classes, usually four classes: masculine, feminine, plant and inanimate. Noun classes are usually marked by prefixes and these prefixes can also show up on adjectives and verbs. Here are examples of noun class agreement in Kunbarlang.

> ### *barbung na-rleng*
> lots of fish
> (lit: fish *masculine*-lots)

> ### *balbarlak ki-rleng*
> lots of crabs
> (lit: crab *feminine*-lots)

> ### *mardugudj ma-rleng*
> lots of plums
> (lit: plum *plant*-lots)

> ### *kuwalak ku-rleng*
> lots of rocks
> (lit: rock *inanimate*-lots)

Aboriginal languages of north-central Top End

North-central Top End languages

These languages represent a 'chain' of languages that are spoken contiguously around the Arnhem Land escarpment; they are 'closer' to each other than the other languages shown here.

Language locations approximate only.

Aboriginal languages of the northwest Top End

TIMOR SEA

Dundas Strait

Cobourg Peninsula

Morrgu
Croker Island

Garrik

Melville Island

Tiwi

Tiwi
Bathurst Island

Van Dieman Gulf

Clarence Strait

Beagle Gulf

Darwin

Wuna

Ngaduk

Limilngan

Palmerston

Larrikiya

Jabiru

Flores

Kungarakany

Batchelor

Bark Hut Inn

Warray

Umbugarla

Adelaide River

Uwinymil

Menhthe

Petjjamalh

Mati Ge

Emmi

Kuwema

Kendjerra-Malh

Marra-Amu

Malak Malak

NORTHERN TERRITORY

Daly River

Kamu

Pine Creek

Marri-syevin

Marra-Nunggu

Matngele

Marri-Thiyel

Marra-Maninjeji

Wagiman

Jawoyn

Wadeye (Port Keats)

Murrinh-Patha

Marri-Ngarr

Marri-Dan

Ngan'gi-Kurunggur

Ngen'gi-Wumirri

Dagoman

Katherine

Joseph Bonaparte Gulf

Murrinh-Kura

Fitzmaurice

Wardaman

Yangman

WESTERN AUSTRALIA

Gajirrang

Jaminjung

Miriwoong

Nungali

Kununurra

Timber Creek

Ngaliwurru

0   10
0   60

■ **Northwest Top End languages**

Language locations approximate only.

WA

NT

QLD

SA

NSW

AUSTRALIA

VIC

TAS

TOP END

Northern Kunwinjkuan languages (Mayali, Kunwinjku, Kunbarlang) have free word order in the sentence and no case endings (ie no markings on nouns to show what their role is in the sentence). All the work of tracking who's doing what to whom is done using the prefixes on verbs. Southern Kunwinjkuan languages (Warray, Jawoyn, Dalabon, Rembarrnga, Ngalakgan, Ngandi and Nunggubuyu), however, have case endings on nouns as well as prefixes on verbs.

Along the coast and the major river systems of the Top End (the Roper in the east, the Daly in the west) there's great diversity among language groups. Like the Kunwinjkuan languages, the languages in this area use complex systems of prefixes on nouns and verbs – note that Yolŋu languages don't, however.

The Daly region

Languages of the Daly region, southwest of Darwin, belong to several groups. Murrinh-Patha (also spelt 'Murrin-Patha') has become one of the more widely spoken languages in the region (see the map opposite). At Wadeye (Port Keats), one of the major communities in the region, members of eight language groups moved in from their traditional countries to live at the mission. Missionaries encouraged the use of Murrinh-Patha, the language of the traditional owners of the country in which the mission was located. A Murrinh-Patha Bible was produced and a dictionary and other documentary materials compiled. Subsequently the school introduced a bilingual education program in Murrinh-Patha.

Partly as a result of these initiatives, Murrinh-Patha gradually became the standard language of the whole community. An unintended side effect has been that few young people now speak any traditional language other than Murrinh-Patha fluently and almost no children understand community languages other than Murrinh-Patha. This is perceived as a serious issue by the community, so the school and the local language centre have recently begun documenting the other community languages.

SOUNDS

Unlike most other Australian languages, the languages of the Daly region have fricative or 'noise' sounds like the English *v* and *z*.

a-dhenirr	frill-necked lizard
	(*dh* is like the *th* in 'there')
a-veng	agile wallaby
a-zjingi	freshwater crocodile
	(*zj* is like the consonant sound in the middle of 'vision')
a-zramu	long-necked turtle
mi-gumbi	white bush apple
	(*g* sounds like a hard *g* prolonged)

STRUCTURE

Languages in the Daly region have a structure typical of prefixing languages, but they make more use of classifiers (words which describe the 'class' a noun falls into – food or animals, for example) than most others. In many Australian languages a generic classifier is used with a specific noun, so that you would say 'vegetable-food yam' rather than just 'yam'. It is possible to use various classifiers with a particular noun to indicate different properties or aspects. For example, in the Mati Ke (or Mati Ge) language of the Wadeye area, the word *marri* means 'cycad', a palm-like plant. If you put the classifier for 'things' in front of it, the combination just refers to the plant. If you use the 'vegetable-food' marker, the meaning is 'ripe cycad nuts'. If you use the 'animal' classifier, it refers to a cockroach that lives in the dead fronds:

awu marri	bush cockroach that lives in dead cycad fronds ('animal' class)
miyi marri	ripe cycad nuts ('food' class)
nhanjdji marri	cycad plant ('thing' class)

Northeast Arnhem

The Aboriginal population in this region is distributed between eight main communities – Ramingining, Milingimbi, Gapuwiyak, Galiwin'ku, Yirrkala, Umbakumba, Angurugu and Numbulwar – and numerous homeland centres. Most non-Aborigines in the region are there for work, either in Aboriginal communities (in schools, clinics and so on) or in the mining towns of Nhulunbuy and Alyangula. As a result of the shift towards self-determination in the 1970s, an increasing number of Aboriginal people hold positions previously dominated by non-Aborigines.

The languages of the northeast corner of Arnhem Land are of the Pama-Nyungan family. They have become commonly known outside the region as the Yolŋu languages. (The o in Yolŋu is pronounced like a long version of the u in 'put'.) In this area, there are some 50 clans and each clan claims to speak a distinct language variety. The relationship of these languages to each other is complex – imagine a patchwork quilt of lands belonging to different clans woven together by spiritual, ceremonial and linguistic threads made by the Ancestral Beings. Land, clan, song, ceremony and languages are all linked together.

One local way of grouping different clan language varieties is to divide languages according to the word they use for 'this' or 'here'. Clans such as Galpu (Gaalpu), Rirratjiŋu (Rirratjingu), Golumala (Guulumala) and Wanŋurri use *dhaŋu* and clans such as Djambarrpuyŋu, Liyagawumirr and Djapu use *dhuwal*. Within the Yolŋu languages (shown on the map on page 195) there are five or six of these larger groupings.

The Yolŋu languages in this northeast corner are surrounded by the non-Pama-Nyungan type. From the northwest these are Burarra, Rembarrnga, Ngandi, Nunggubuyu on the mainland and Anindilyakwa, the language of Groote Eylandt. To this day groups within a geographical area intermarry and children are raised with different languages spoken around the hearth. In all communities the population is still multilingual, and almost all languages in the region still have speakers. The comments following should be understood in light of this fact. However, some have very few speakers and the population of speakers of several varieties is ageing.

The most widely spoken Yolŋu varieties are, from west to east: Djinaŋ, spoken around Ramingining; a Dhuwal variety usually referred to as Djambarrpuyŋu (but somewhat different to the traditional Djambarrpuyŋu) spoken from Milingimbi to Gapuwiyak; and Dhuwaya, a koine (a new Yolŋu language) that has evolved around Yirrkala. At Numbulwar, Kriol is the first language of most young people but there's a major effort being undertaken in the community to maintain other languages, particularly Nunggubuyu. Anindilyakwa is still the first language of indigenous people on Groote Eylandt.

Traditional languages and culture are being supported by the schools in the region through various activities and programs. There are increasing numbers of Aboriginal teachers who can be proactive about local language issues. The maintenance of languages under threat is made easier by the fact that people still have extensive passive understanding of them – that is, they can understand the languages even if they can't speak them fluently. Three communities have formal bilingual programs in which children are taught in English and local languages.

The Yolŋu have also always encouraged people living in their communities to learn their languages. This ethos was even supported during the mission period – the mission expected staff to learn something of a local language.

Languages of the area have been written since the 1960s. Most writing is still associated with schools and Bible translation. Bilingual schools have printing facilities so this is where most locally produced material can be found. Some of these materials are available at local craft shops and newsagencies. Others are part of the Northern Australian Collection at the State Library of the Northern Territory in Darwin. The Yolŋu languages share a common orthography, but different writing systems exist for the non-Pama-Nyungan languages of the region.

Aboriginal languages of northeast Arnhem Land

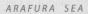

ARAFURA SEA

WESSEL ISLANDS • Marchinbar Is

Drysdale Is

Nhaŋu • Guluwuru Is

Mooroongga Is • Yaŋ-nhaŋu
Yabooma Is
Milingimbi • Howard Is

Nhaŋu • Elcho Is
Galiwinku

Burarra • Djinaŋ

Dhaŋu

Inglis Is

Dhuwal • Dhuwala
Raminginiŋ

Dhuwal

Arnhem
Bay

Dhuwul • Dhawal
• Nhulunbuy
Dhuwala • Yirrkala

Djinaŋ • Dhuwala
Dhuwal

Dhaŋu

Djinba • Gapuwiyak • Dhuwala

Dha'yi

Dhaŋu • Dhaŋu

Dhuwula

Ritharrŋu

ARNHEM LAND

Dhuwula

Dha'yi

Dhuwal

• Garrthalala

Rembarrnga

Dhuwala

NORTHERN
TERRITORY

Ritharrŋu

GULF OF
Isle CARPENTARIA
Woodah

Ngandi

Anindilyakwa
Milyakburra
Bickerton • Alyangula • Umbakumba

• Bulman

Nunggubuyu

Is

GROOTE
Angurugu EYLANDT

Nyundi

Anindilyakwa

• Numbulwar

0 ———— 60 km
0 ———— 30 mi

■ Northeast Arnhem Land languages
■ Yolŋu languages

Language locations approximate only.

Based on a map supplied by the Northern
Territory Department of Education.

AUSTRALIA

WA
NT
SA
QLD
NSW
VIC
TAS

Northeast Arnhem

195

FURTHER READING

For further information on Aboriginal languages of the region, you can contact the Katherine Regional Language Centre, Diwurruwurru-jaru (www.kathlangcentre.org.au, telephone 08 8971 1233).

SIL Darwin (formerly the Summer Institute of Linguistics) has published many academic works and vernacular readers, both secular and religious, in a large number of indigenous Australian languages. Contact SIL for more information at PMB 1, Berrimah, 0828, telephone 08 8922 5700.

There are two broad types of language in Western Australia. Those spoken in the Kimberley, roughly north of the Fitzroy River, are of the prefixing type, like the languages of the Top End of the Northern Territory. The remainder are purely suffixing (see page 141 for details on suffixing and prefixing).

The southwest

A single language, Nyungar, was spoken in the southwest of the state and existed in a number of different dialects. In the early days of contact with Europeans, a large number of loanwords were taken into English. However, the effects of European settlement then caused a catastrophic loss of language (and culture), and there are now very few fluent speakers of Nyungar remaining.

The Murchison & Gascoyne

The main surviving language of this region is Wajarri, originally spoken in the Eastern Murchison. Although there were a number of different languages spoken in this area, the people all refer to themselves as Yamaji and will say that they speak the Yamaji language. Wajarri is also spoken in Carnarvon where the original languages are essentially moribund. The eastern Wajarri people live in the Western Desert cultural area.

Pilbara

The southern and western Pilbara region, from the Gascoyne to the Ashburton river, formed a cultural area with the languages spoken along the Pilbara coast. The languages of this region also had similarities but, sadly, few speakers remain.

A number of languages are still spoken in the northern and eastern Pilbara, the most widely known being Yindjibarndi, spoken in Roebourne, Onslow and other Pilbara towns. The Pilbara people form a cultural group sharing similar kinship systems and ritual practices. People travel from Carnarvon in the south to Jigalong in the east and La Grange mission in the north for summer ceremonies.

Western Desert

Dialects of the Western Desert language are spoken across large parts of inland Western Australia and adjacent parts of South Australia and the Northern Territory. In Western Australia this language extends from near the Great Australian Bight, north to the Kimberley and west to the Hamersley Ranges and Murchison goldfields.

Kimberley

There were originally about 15 different prefixing languages spoken in the Kimberley region. There are marked differences in vocabulary between most of these, and they are classified as belonging to eight different language families. The languages of the remaining areas of Western Australia all belong to the Pama-Nyungan family.

Most Aboriginal people over the age of 30 in the Kimberley, Pilbara and Western Desert regions speak one or more traditional languages. Throughout most of the state, Aboriginal people, except possibly the elderly, also speak English. There's an array of varieties of Aboriginal English, ranging from close to standard Australian English, through to varieties very close to Kriol (see page 170).

The effects of European settlement

The European settlement of Western Australia began with the establishment of the Swan River colony (Perth) in 1829 and spread to other parts of the state over the next 50 years, with agriculture and the pastoral industry, pearl fishing on the Pilbara and Kimberley coasts, and gold rushes in the Kalgoorlie and Murchison regions. The effects of European settlement on Aboriginal languages vary from a gradual decline in use over a number of generations, to rapid and complete extinction.

Knowledge of the Nyungar language of the southwest corner of the state has been gradually declining for 150 years. Today, younger Nyungar people may know little more than a few hundred words and a handful of phrases. These are used to replace English words in what is otherwise a variety of Aboriginal English. The original dialect diversity of Nyungar has been compromised, with virtually nothing remaining of the Perth dialect, and most people using words of the eastern Nyungar areas.

English has also had an influence on the sound system and grammatical structure of modern Nyungar. The initial nasal sounds *ng* and *ny* are not used by younger speakers, who pronounce words like *nguup* (blood) as *nuup*, and Nyungar itself is now called 'Noongar'. Younger speakers also use word order to distinguish the subject and object, rather than using the case-marking system of traditional Nyungar.

Language loss in other areas has been more catastrophic. Most of the languages originally spoken along the Ashburton river are now extinct, not because their speakers have shifted more and more to English, but because whole communities were destroyed as a result of European settlement. The languages did not die, their speakers did.

In some places, as elsewhere in Australia, speakers of different languages were thrown together in organised settlements. Languages were then lost as people shifted to one or two main languages away from their mother tongues. Yindjibarndi is the most successful survivor of the many languages which came together in Roebourne. As in other parts of northern Australia, a new language (called Kriol) arose in parts of the Kimberley using words borrowed mainly from English, but with a sound system and some aspects of grammar taken from traditional languages.

Keeping languages strong

In recent years, many West Australian communities have increased efforts to maintain their languages and, in some cases, to revive languages which have been lost. An important part of this effort has been the establishment of community language centres that provide general language resource materials. The language centres encourage the interest of members of the general public and welcome visitors. Language centres are located in Perth, Kalgoorlie, Bunbury, Geraldton, Northam, Port Hedland, Halls Creek and Kununurra.

Until recently, Western Australia did not have a policy promoting the teaching of Australian languages in state-run schools and most language teaching or bilingual education programmes were community-based and privately or federally funded. Now, however, there is a framework for teaching Aboriginal languages in primary schools and for promoting language awareness. Hopefully this will not only aid language retention, but also lead to awareness of Aboriginal languages in the general non-Aboriginal community.

Language maintenance and revival is closely tied to cultural maintenance and revival, so an important aspect of this is sustaining a spiritual connection to the land. In recent times, communities have sought increased control over their traditional lands. In some areas people have moved back to their homelands and established out-stations; in other places Aboriginal community groups hold pastoral leases and so retain access to their land for traditional purposes alongside the land being used to run stock. Aboriginal rangers are increasingly involved in the management of national parks, and many communities continue to seek their rights to Native Title under federal and state law.

Specific locations

The legacy of the Nyungar people is clearest to visitors in the host of local names for places, plants and animals found in the southwest. Aboriginal heritage trails giving details of the uses of various plants, the habits of animals and historical and mythological information can be found in most national parks throughout the area. In the Goldfields, in communities across the Nullarbor Plain and in the desert, and along the Canning Stock Route north to the Kimberley, people speak dialects of the Western Desert language.

In the Pilbara, the gorges in Karijini, the Hamersley Ranges National Park, are a popular travel destination. This is Panyjima, Kurrama and Yinhawangka country. The Millstream/Chichester Ranges National Park is Kurrama and Yindjibarndi country. Aboriginal rangers from these local groups work in the parks, while local Aboriginal groups organise wilderness tours of Karijini, led by local experts.

Broome has speakers of Yawuru and probably also Karajarri, a Western Desert language. Cape Leveque has a population of the seagoing Bardi people. The Gibb River road passes mainly through Ngarinyin country, and the Bungle Bungle National Park, south of Turkey Creek, has Kija and Jaru speakers. Miriwoong is spoken further to the north, around Kununurra and Lake Argyle on the Ord River.

In the north of the state, especially in the desert, in the Pilbara and Kimberley, Aboriginal people often speak the new language, Kriol, or Aboriginal English.

Aboriginal languages of Western Australia

■ **Western Australian languages**

Language locations approximate only.

Language use

Aboriginal people don't usually expect to speak their languages with non-Aboriginal people and in most such situations English is the language of choice. However, travellers who choose to try out a few local names for animals, plants or places, will convey the message that they are interested in Aboriginal languages and sympathetic to Aboriginal culture.

Aboriginal English isn't always easily understood by speakers of other English dialects (see the box on page 170). Visitors shouldn't try to speak Kriol or Aboriginal English, however – because of the negative connotations of 'pidgin English', such attempts might be seen as patronising and insulting.

Place names

The list below is composed of names from the Pilbara:

Jajiwurra	Robe River
Japurakunha	Marillana Gorge
Jintawirrina	Millstream Station
Kalharramunha	Rio Tinto Gorge
Karijini	Hamersley Range (National Park)
Karlayanguyinha	Cowera Gorge
Kartirtikunha	Yampire Gorge
Kawuyu	Mt Nicholson
Mangkurtu	Fortescue River
Mukuriyarra	Mt Murray
Murlunmunyjurna	Crossing Pool
Ngampiku	Wittenoom (Gorge)
Pajinhurrpa	Cossak
Parrkapinya	Whim Creek
Partiikunha	Clamina Gorge
Pilirripinha	Manyjina Gorge
Plrnayinmurru	Mt Brockman
Pirtan	Onslow

Punurrunha	Mt Bruce
Walkartatharra	Mt Alexander
Yirramakartu	Roebourne, Jubilee Pool

Many place names in the southwest of the state end in *-up*. These are all original Nyungar names and the ending simply indicates that the word is the name of a place. Some examples of towns with this ending are:

Boyanup	Jerramungup	Nannup
Cowaramup	Kirrup	Porongurup
Dandalup	Kojonup	Quinninup
Dardenup	Manjimup	Wagerup
Gnowangerup	Mungallup	Wok-alup

In the wheatbelt (southwest Western Australia), a good number of place names end in *-n* or *-ng*. These are also Nyungar names. Some towns with this kind of name are:

Burracoppin	Kellerberrin	Popanyinning
Corrigin	Kondinin	Quairading
Cunderdin	Merredin	Tammin
Katanning	Narrogin	Woodanilling

While some of these place names most likely 'meant something' rather than simply being names, it's not possible to know what this was without detailed knowledge of the named place and the mythology surrounding it. Resemblances to other Nyungar words are no guarantee of a connection in meaning.

The southeast of Australia, comprising the present-day areas of Victoria, Tasmania, New South Wales and the Australian Capital Territory (ACT), was settled early and intensively. When the British intruders and their descendants spread across the country, the original inhabitants were dispossessed of their land and killed in large numbers through battle, the spread of disease, and the destruction of their environment and means of living. People were also herded onto missions and government settlements, sometimes being forced to live with their enemies, and their traditional ways of life were prohibited. As a result, there was only partial transmission of traditional Aboriginal culture and language from one generation to the next, and a great deal of knowledge was lost.

Today, in New South Wales, a few old fluent speakers remain for a small number of languages, including Bundjalung of the north coast around Lismore, and Baagandji, spoken on the Darling River near Wilcannia. There are no living full speakers of a Victorian Aboriginal language, and none of the Victorian languages is used as the main means of communication in any community. However, many Aboriginal people carefully preserve some elements of their linguistic heritage, even generations after the last fluent speakers have passed away. Today, words from traditional languages can still be heard in Melbourne and Sydney, and in country areas of New South Wales and Victoria. In many communities there's rising interest in traditional languages and culture, and efforts are under way to preserve and maintain the knowledge that remains, and to augment it from written sources.

Aboriginal languages of Victoria, New South Wales and ACT

QUEENSLAND

SOUTH AUSTRALIA

NEW SOUTH WALES

Darling

Lachlan

Murrum

VICTORIA

TASMAN
SEA

Bundjalung

Gumbaynggir

Gamilaraay

Baagandji

Ngiyambaa

Dharuk

Sydney

Wemba
Wemba

Wiradjuri

Canberra

ACT

Yorta Yorta

Thagung-
wurrung

Woiwurrung

Watha-
wurrung

Melbourne

Muk Thang

Warrnambool

Great Dividing Range

King
Island

Bass Strait

Flinders
Island

0 — 250 km
0 — 150 mi

■ **Victorian, NSW & ACT languages**
Language locations approximate only.

NT   QLD

WA   SA   NSW

AUSTRALIA   VIC

TAS

Visitors to the southeastern states will see evidence of traditional Aboriginal languages in three areas:

- the continuing use of Aboriginal words and expressions by Aboriginal people
- names for places and features of the landscape
- Aboriginal words that have entered the English language and are in common use by all Australians

Victoria

The language that covered the area north from Melbourne almost to Echuca on the Murray River is known as Woiwurrung (for the dialect south of the Great Dividing Range) or Thagungwurrung (for the northern dialect). Other important languages of Victoria include Wathawurrung, spoken near Geelong, Wemba Wemba of northwestern Victoria, the Warrnambool language from southwestern Victoria, Yorta Yorta around the Murray east of Echuca, and Muk Thang, the language of the Ganai (also spelled Kurnai) of Gippsland.

Melbourne was first settled by Europeans in 1835, and within a few years the Aboriginal population was largely destroyed. From 1863 the survivors were placed in a reserve at Coranderrk, near Healesville, and later at other reserves such as Lake Tyers in Gippsland and Framlingham near Warrnambool in the Western District. In the 1960s, linguist Luise Hercus carried out an extensive survey of the whole state to record what could be gleaned of the traditional languages – the result was a book containing outline descriptions of three languages from northwestern Victoria and adjacent areas of New South Wales, plus word lists for a number of other languages. For most of the state our knowledge comes from word lists and very brief notes on language structures recorded by settlers, administrators and missionaries in the late 19th century.

In general, Aboriginal words tend to end in vowels, but a feature of Victorian languages is the use of a wide variety of consonants at the end of words. This is reflected in some of the plant names borrowed into English from Victorian languages, such as **ballart** (native cherry) and **murrnong** or **myrnong** (yam-daisy), and in the names of places such as Koowee-rup and Gariwerd. (The latter is an Aboriginal name that's been reintroduced as an alternative name for the Grampians, a mountain range in western Victoria.) For many place names it's impossible to give an exact meaning because of the lack of reliable information; however, following are some names for which the meaning is clear:

Allambee	mishearing of **ngalambi** 'to remain, dwell' – town near Yarragon, Gippsland and Yallambie, a suburb of Melbourne
Boort	'smoke' – town in Mallee, northwestern Victoria
Coranderrk	Victorian 'Christmas bush', a small flowering tree – place near Healesville
Geelong	'tongue' – town to the west of Melbourne
Korrumburra	'march fly' – town in Gippsland
Lara	'stone' – town north of Geelong
Leongatha	'our teeth' – town in Gippsland
Mirboo	'kidney' – town in Gippsland
Narre Warren	'red' – suburb southeast of Melbourne
Wollert	'possum' – place north of Melbourne
Wonthaggi	'Fetch!' – town on the Gippsland coast

The following are some other words in Victorian languages that have entered the English language: **bunyip** (a mythical swamp-dwelling creature), **yabby** (a crustacean), **cumbungi** (bulrush), **dillon bush** (a plant), **lerp** (a form of scale), **lowan** (mallee fowl) and **tuan** (gliding possum).

Further information on the indigenous languages of Victoria can be obtained from the Victorian Aboriginal Corporation for Languages, 295 King St, Melbourne. Their library is open from 9am to 5pm each weekday. Go to www.vaclang.org.au.

Tasmania

The British takeover of Tasmania began in 1803 and most of the indigenous population was wiped out within 50 years or so. There were about a dozen Tasmanian languages and it is interesting to note that there are no clear resemblances between Tasmanian languages and those of the mainland. No full speakers survived into the 20th century, but partial knowledge lingered on, and along with written sources this is providing the basis for teaching Palawa Kani – meaning 'Tassie blackfellas talk' – to Aboriginal children in schools. Unfortunately, records of Tasmania's languages consist almost entirely of word lists. These have been collected and published by NJB Plomley as *A Word List of the Tasmanian Aboriginal Languages*.

New South Wales

Current knowledge of the traditional languages of New South Wales is much richer than knowledge of the languages in Victoria and Tasmania. Around Sydney and the central coast, which was settled by Europeans from 1788, the only available information is from 18th- and 19th-century records, mainly short word lists. However, for a number of other languages, especially those of inland New South Wales and the north coast, there are tape recordings, grammars and dictionaries compiled by linguists who worked with the last generation of fluent speakers.

Languages for which there's a great deal of reliable information available include Bundjalung and Gumbaynggir (north coast), Gamilaraay (also spelled Kamilaroi), Ngiyambaa (or Wangaaybuwan), Wiradjuri (all inland New South Wales), and Baagandji (or Paakantyi, far west). Speakers of some of these languages remain and there are efforts under way in Aboriginal communities to revive and preserve linguistic and cultural heritage.

Throughout New South Wales, as in Victoria, there are numerous place names that have an Aboriginal origin.

It's possible to give the literal translation for many of these (although information on the significance of these names in the mythology and culture is often not available). Here are some examples giving the original pronunciation and meaning:

Boggabilla	'bagaaybila'	place full of creeks
Bundarra	'bundaarra'	place of kangaroos
Cobar	'gubarr'	red ochre
Coonamble	'gunambil'	full of excrement
Gunnedah	'gunithaa'	orphan
Nambucca	'bagabaga'	knees
Torrowotto	'thuru-katu'	snake's windbreak
Uralla	'urala'	camp
Wagga Wagga	'waagan-waagan'	crows
Woolgoolga	'wiigulga'	black fig tree

Dozens of words from New South Wales languages are now part of general Australian English, especially the names of plants and animals that were new to the first European settlers. These include:

animals	dingo; koala; wallaby; wallaroo
artefacts	coolamon (bark dish); woomera (spear-thrower); nulla-nulla (club); gunya (shelter)
birds	galah; kookaburra; brolga; currawong; budgerigar
landscape	billabong (river pool); gibber (stone)
plants	mulga; coolabah; gidgee; bindi-eye

Australian Capital Territory

Canberra, which occupies part of the traditional land of the Ngunnawal people, contains the principal repository for data on Aboriginal culture, namely the Australian Institute of Aboriginal and Torres Strait Islander Studies. It's adjacent to the Australian Museum, and the library is open to the public on weekdays (except Tuesdays). Details are available at www.aiatsis.gov.au.

The first British settlement in Queensland was a penal colony established at Moreton Bay in 1824 and moved to the site of Brisbane in 1825. By the end of the 19th century European settlers had taken over the whole of Queensland. Those Aboriginal people who were not killed in frontier battles were unable to continue their traditional way of life, and were forced to accept work, largely unpaid, on rural properties. Under the Protection Act of 1897 any Aboriginal person could be declared a ward of the state, and people were forcibly interned on reserves, sometimes in places remote from their country and people, such as Palm Island.

Present-day Queensland

Present-day Aboriginal people in Queensland often refer to themselves as *murries — murry* is the word for 'man' in many of the languages of southern Queensland (including Bidjara and Diri — see the map on page 213). In Brisbane there is the Murri Court, a Magistrates Court which is responsible for sentencing Aboriginal offenders. This court has Murri elders as advisers and takes into account cultural issues when determining appropriate penalties.

Given that Aboriginal people were unable to retain their traditional way of life, it's not surprising that by the middle of the 20th century there were scores of Queensland languages of which only a few elderly speakers had a full knowledge. However, languages do not die suddenly, and the last full speakers were succeeded by a generation of people with at least some knowledge of the language. Among the present generation there has been a resurgence of interest in language, and currently strenuous efforts are being made by many communities to preserve their language where some knowledge remains or to restore it from written materials. In Mitchell, for instance, Aboriginal children are introduced to the Gunggari language at school.

Cape York

Cape York remained an exception. In that area there was less European intrusion and traditional life and languages have been better maintained. Languages that have survived in the Cape York area include Koko Pera (also spelt 'Berra') on the west coast of the peninsula south of the Mitchell River, and the Wik languages of the Aurukun area further to the north. Kuku Yalanji, a language of the Bloomfield River area south of Cooktown, is still spoken. Guugu Yimidhirr (also spelt 'Guugu Yimithirr'), the language of the area just to the north of Cooktown, is still spoken, but the language of younger speakers is somewhat modified and influenced by English. This is a common phenomenon. *Koko*, *Kuku* and *Guugu* are, by the way, different spellings of the same word, which means 'language'.

ROCK ART IN QUEENSLAND   Philip Morrissey

Some of Australia's largest rock art sites are found in Queensland. The escarpment country surrounding Laura is famed for its distinctive paintings of Quinkans (spirit beings). The area was first discovered by Europeans in the 19th century, with further discoveries in 1959. Postcontact art is also featured, including representations of the hated Native Police – it's thought the artists were attempting to counter the menace of European settlement with magic. Another significant site is Carnarvon Gorge in Carnarvon National Park, which has hundreds of paintings and engravings.

Aboriginal languages of Queensland

- **Queensland languages**

Language locations approximate only.

The Yimidhirr people have a particular claim to fame – they gave the word *kangaroo* to English and ultimately to other languages. The Yimidhirr first encountered Europeans when Captain Cook beached the *Endeavour* for repairs in 1770. Members of Cook's party elicited some vocabulary including *kangaroo*. Later some doubt was cast on the authenticity of this word, but it is definitely a Guugu Yimidhirr word. The form is actually *kang-u-rru*, with the *ng* pronounced as in 'singer', not as in 'finger'.

The Yagara language of the Brisbane area has also provided Australian English with a number of words, including several that are not easily recognisable as Aboriginal words. These include *dilly* (as in 'dilly bag'), *bung* (in 'go bung', meaning 'cease to function'), *yakka* 'hard work' and *humpy* 'hut', though the last of these has been distorted somewhat from the original, which is *ngumpi*.

Thirty years ago you could travel around Queensland without coming across many references to the traditional owners of the land in the tourist literature, and there were few sites where one could see Aboriginal culture. Today, however, there are a number of cultural sites such as the Tjapukai Aboriginal Cultural Park north of Cairns, the Jubinara Aboriginal Art Gallery in Townsville, and the Kalkadoon Tribal Council and Cultural Keeping Place in Mount Isa. In the nature of things these venues feature artefacts rather than language, but there are elders available who like to discuss language.

The first official British settlement in South Australia was established on the site of Adelaide in 1836, though whalers and sealers had been living on Kangaroo Island since the early 1800s and kidnapping Aboriginal women to live with them. European settlement had spread over the whole state by the 1870s, though only sparsely in the dry north and west of the state. However, the establishment of stock routes, the Overland Telegraph and railways brought Europeans into even these remote areas, which otherwise might have escaped significant European contact. As in other parts of Australia Aboriginal people were killed in punitive expeditions and fell prey to introduced diseases; many of the survivors were herded into missions.

Regional langauges

As might be expected, the survival of Aboriginal people and their languages in South Australia largely relates to the intensity of white settlement. In the southeast corner of the state, the Buandik (or Bunganditj) people were driven to near extinction and their language is known only from early records. In contrast, dialects of the Western Desert language are still spoken in the far northwest of the state, including Pitjantjatjara and Yankutjatjara. Kukata, a more southerly language, no longer has full speakers. In between these extremes there are a score of languages that have ceased to be in regular use. The Kaurna people of the Adelaide Plains were the first to lose their lands to the intruders, though the language survived into the early 20th century. The Ngarrindjeri people living around the mouth of the Murray retained their language, Yaralde, up to the 1950s. Further north and west are a number of languages that have lost their last full speakers over the last few decades. These include Diyari, Arabana, and Wirangu.

FLINDERS RANGES DREAMING

The 'spirit of place', almost palpable in the Flinders Ranges, has inspired a rich heritage of Dreaming stories. Many of these are secret, but others related by Adnyamathanha Elders explain the creation of the landscape and the native birds and animals that inhabit it.

Arkaroola comes from Arkaroo, the name of the Dreaming Serpent Ancestor. Suffering from a powerful thirst, Arkaroo drank Lake Frome dry, then dragged his bloated body back into the ranges, carving out the sinuous Arkaroola Creek as he went. He went underground to sleep, but all that salty water gave him a belly ache. Now he constantly moves about to relieve the pain – the reason for the 30 to 40 small earth tremors that occur in the area every year.

Another story relates that the walls of Ikara (Wilpena Pound) are the bodies of two Akurra (giant snakes), who coiled around Ikara during an initiation ceremony, creating a whirlwind during which they devoured most of the participants.

There's also a story that explains why crows are black: the bossy eagle Wildu sought revenge on his nephews, who had tried to kill him by building a great fire. All the birds were caught in the flames, and, originally white, they emerged blackened and burnt. The magpies and willy wagtails were partially scorched, but the crows were entirely blackened, and have remained so to this day.

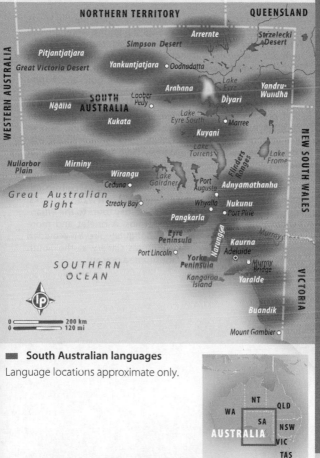

Aboriginal languages of South Australia

South Australian languages

Language locations approximate only.

Present-day South Australia

Today, over most of South Australia Aboriginal people speak various forms of Aboriginal English. In the area around Adelaide and to the south this is called 'Nunga English' – *nunga* is a word for 'Aborigine' taken from the Streaky Bay area. The vocabulary is mainly from English, but includes some Aboriginal words such as *bandabri* 'gun' and *kappa* 'tobacco' from Kaurna, and *marra* 'hand' and *guna* 'faeces', which are found in a large number of Australian languages.

At present, as in other areas, there is a strong move to maintain Aboriginal languages that are still living and to restore and reclaim those that are no longer in regular use. The Kaurna people, for instance, have a strong sense of identity and are now attempting to revive their language on the basis of early records.

An opportunity for an experience of Aboriginal culture and language is available from Desert Tracks (www.deserttracks. com.au), who operate three- and five-day tours to the Pitjantjatjara Homelands from Alice Springs. A briefer and more easily accessible introduction to Aboriginal culture is provided by the Australian Aboriginal Cultures Gallery at the South Australian Museum (www.samuseum.sa.gov.au).

There are three Torres Strait Islander languages, and they're spoken by a population that is of largely Melanesian, but also European, Asian and Aboriginal, background. Their homelands are a group of small islands scattered along the waterway known as Torres Strait, between the tip of Cape York and Papua New Guinea (see the map on page 221).

Two of the Torres Strait Islander languages are original indigenous languages. Kala Lagaw Ya (KLY) is spoken by the people of the western islands of Saibai (and thus now in Seisia and Bamaga), Dauan, Boigu, Mabuiag, Muralag, Badu, Moa (Kubin) and Narupai, and the central islands of Masig, Purma, Yam and Warraber. Meriam Mir (MM) is spoken by the people from the eastern islands of Mer (where it is primarily spoken by adults), Erub and Ugar. Kala Lagaw Ya is believed to be related to Australian Aboriginal languages. Meriam Mir, on the other hand, belongs to the Trans Fly family of languages along the Papuan coast.

The third indigenous language of Torres Strait Islanders is an English-based creole called Torres Strait Broken (TSB). It's an established lingua franca, mainly spoken in the eastern and central Islands and Thursday Island, and is the first language of most people there who were born after World War II. Nevertheless, most adults also maintain their traditional languages.

Thursday Island has a mixed community of European, Asian and Aboriginal people. English is an official language and is used extensively in government offices, schools, churches, hospitals, shops and so on. The two indigenous languages are often used by their speakers among themselves, but Torres Strait Broken, as mentioned, is the most commonly used language on the island.

There are about 30,000 Torres Strait Islanders, but only about 6000 still live in the Torres Strait. The remaining 80% have moved to towns and cities in the mainland of Australia for various reasons – mainly for jobs, good health and better education for their children. Most Torres Strait Islanders who have decided to move to the mainland have settled in the coastal towns and cities of Queensland.

Despite exposure to the dominant western culture and English language, Torres Strait Islanders on the mainland have managed to maintain their traditional languages exceptionally well, with the help of various programmes. (Details are available from the Federation of Aboriginal and Torres Strait Islander Languages at www.fatsil.org.) Kala Lagaw Ya has about 3000 speakers, while there are around 2000 Meriam Mir speakers, and all Torres Strait Islanders speak Torres Strait Broken, regardless of where they live in Australia.

European contact

European contact has had devastating effects on the Torres Strait languages and culture. The colonisation process and cruel policies of assimilation, segregation and integration have greatly contributed to the marginalisation of Torres Strait Islander culture and languages. There were official limitations on the use of indigenous languages in schools and public places.

The creation of Torres Strait Broken was one result of colonisation. It was developed mainly from the Pacific Island pidgin called Bislama, which was brought to Torres Strait by Pacific Islanders working in the area's marine industry. Other migrant groups, such as Japanese, Malays and Chinese, also had an influence, and Torres Strait Broken is now distinctly different from Bislama.

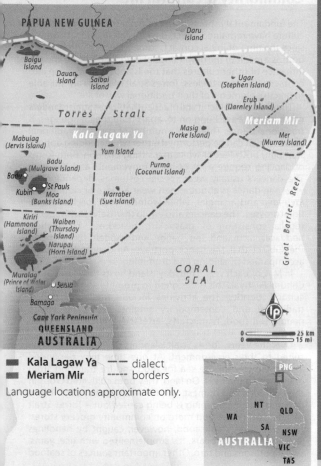

Torres Strait
inhabited islands & linguistic boundaries

PAPUA NEW GUINEA

Daru
Island

Boigu
Island

Dauan   Saibai
Island   Island

Ugar
(Stephen Island)

Erub
(Darnley Island)

Torres Strait

Meriam Mir

Kala Lagaw Ya

Masig
(Yorke Island)

Mer
(Murray Island)

Mabuiag
(Jervis Island)

Yum Island

Badu
(Mulgrave Island)

Purma
(Coconut Island)

Badu

St Pauls

Kubin   Moa
(Banks Island)

Warraber
(Sue Island)

Kiriri
(Hammond
Island)

Waiben
(Thursday
Island)

Great Barrier Reef

Narupai
(Horn Island)

Muralag
(Prince of Wales
Island)

Seisia

CORAL
SEA

Bamaga

Cape York Peninsula

QUEENSLAND
AUSTRALIA

0   25 km
0   15 mi

■ Kala Lagaw Ya   — — dialect
■ Meriam Mir   ······ borders

Language locations approximate only.

PNG

NT   QLD
WA
SA   NSW
AUSTRALIA   VIC
TAS

Community & cultural life

The fundamental aspects of the original Torres Strait Islander culture have remained intact, despite colonisation. However, since the time of initial contact, some aspects have changed, both as a result of the dominance of European culture and the influence of other cultures that the Islanders have come into contact with. Nevertheless, Torres Strait Islanders are still able to practise elements of their traditional way of life.

The most notable cultural practice that Torres Strait Islanders on all islands have hung on to, apart from their languages, is traditional dance. There are a number of styles of traditional dance, which can be performed either while standing upright stamping both feet or while in a sitting position. Both forms of dancing require a lot of hand movements and jumping. The dancers usually wear special costumes, depending on what the dance is about – men wear a piece of cloth called *lava-lava* and a singlet, while women wear specially made floral dresses. The dancers also equip themselves with special regalia consisting of grass-skirt, headdress, headbands, necklaces, arm and leg bands and models representing the subject that the dance portrays. All dances are usually accompanied by singing and drumming.

In May of each year, Thursday Island hosts the Torres Strait Cultural Festival. This is designed to promote and strengthen cultural identity. The activities include traditional dance, traditional and contemporary singing, and stalls where people sell food, handicrafts, artefacts and carvings of all descriptions.

Over the years, Torres Strait Islanders developed a lifestyle suited to their environment. At one time they depended almost entirely on the sea for food and for transport from one island to the next. On land, they both cultivated crops in their gardens and domesticated animals, mainly pigs. These days not much gardening is being carried out – Torres Strait Islanders rely more and more on community grocery stores. Fish is still the staple food, however, caught by handlines and nets or hand spears. It's supplemented with rice, yams, sweet potatoes and taro. Other important sources of seafood are dugong and turtle, which are hunted in the traditional way with a special harpoon. (Both dugong and turtle are considered a luxury, and are only eaten on special occasions like weddings and tombstone unveilings.)

For special occasions, Torres Strait Islanders hold traditional feasts which include dancing, singing and lots of food. Traditional food requires a lot of preparation. One of the popular traditional foods, for example, is *sop-sop*, a mixture of vegetables chopped into small pieces and cooked in coconut cream. For just about every feast, food is cooked in an earth oven or *kap mauri*. The food all kinds of things, including vegetables, pig, dugong and damper – is prepared and wrapped, then placed on hot stones lying on the bottom of a specially dug pit.

Tombstone unveiling is one of the important family events celebrated with a big traditional feast. The family of the deceased person collects money from each member of the family before the ceremony, erects a tombstone on the grave and puts on the feast.

The outer island communities are changing fairly rapidly from traditional villages to small townships. All the islands now have modern houses, schools, medical facilities, telephones and electricity. However, in general, life on the islands proceeds at a notably leisurely pace. The daily activities of the people revolve around family and community affairs.

Torres Strait Islanders are devout Christians, and most belong to the Anglican church, though some islands have smaller churches of other denominations. Church services are normally conducted in English but most of the hymns are sung in the indigenous languages.

An important religious event that people throughout the Torres Strait celebrate on 1 July each year is the festival of the 'Coming of the Light'. This festival celebrates the arrival of the missionaries of the London Missionary Society in the Torres Strait in 1871. The festival usually consists of a church service followed by a re-enactment of how the people on each island greeted the missionaries.

The main authorities in an island community are the community council chairperson and the councillors, the priest and the clan elders. Visitors are expected to observe cultural protocol when visiting the islands, so it's important to find out as much as possible beforehand.

On the islands

The places that are visited most frequently by outsiders are Bamaga, Seisia and Thursday Island. In winter, tourists travel by road to Cape York and camp in the camping area at Seisia. A regular ferry operates from Thursday Island to the Northern Peninsula Area communities on most days of the week.

Thursday Island is the commercial and administrative centre of Torres Strait, and has a fascinating history as a defence outpost in the late 19th century. At the fort on Green Hill there are 16-inch cannons which were built during that era in fear of a Russian invasion that never eventuated.

All the Torres Strait islands not included in the Muralag (Prince of Wales) group, including Thursday Island, are referred to as outer islands. If you're thinking of visiting any of the outer islands, it's important to make an arrangement with the council of the island – accommodation is limited.

Dialects

KALA LAGAW YA

Kala Lagaw Ya (KLY) is a language with four dialects:

- the Kala Kawaw Ya (KKY) of the islands of Saibai, Dauan and Boigu
- Mabuiag (M) of Mabuiag Island and Badu
- Kaurareg (K) of Kubin (Moa)
- Nurapai (Horn Island)

The differences between these dialects are minimal and lie mainly in words and sounds.

MERIAM MIR

Meriam Mir (MM) had two dialects and the differences between them were restricted to words and sounds. Sadly, only the Mer dialect has survived.

TORRES STRAIT BROKEN

As in the Kriol spoken in the Top End, the vocabulary of Torres Strait Broken varies quite widely, with different words being derived from the indigenous languages in the eastern and central/western islands. For example:

Awa, yumi go.   Uncle, let's go. (Eastern)
Awadhe, yumi go.   Uncle, let's go. (Central/Western)

Sounds

VOWELS

The vowels in the three Torres Strait Islander languages resemble those of English. The simple vowels are:

- *a* as in 'but'
- *e* as in 'pet'
- *i* as in 'bit'
- *o* as in 'pot'
- *u* as in 'put'

The diphthongs are:

- *ei* as in 'pay'
- *ai* as in 'aisle'
- *oi* as in 'toy'
- *au* as in 'now'
- *eu* pronounced like 'milk' in Cockney English

Kala Lagaw Ya also has an unstressed vowel that sounds similar to how the two *a* sounds are pronounced in the English word 'arena'.

CONSONANTS

All the Torres Strait languages have the consonant sounds *b*, *d*, *g*, *j*, *k*, *l*, *m*, *n*, *p*, *r*, *s*, *t*, *w*, *y* and *z*, as in English. Kala Lagaw Ya has three additional consonant sounds, *dh* as in 'the', *ng* as in 'swing' and *th* as in 'thin'.

Pronouns

You'll notice in the table below that there are four forms of the pronoun 'we', and two forms of the plural 'you' and 'they'. There's a basic distinction here between the forms that refer to just two people and those that refer to more than two – for 'we', there are also forms that include the person being spoken to versus forms that exclude him or her.

	Kala Lagaw Ya	Meriam Mir	TSB
I	ngay; ngath	kaka	ai
you sg	ngi; ngidh; ni; nidh	mama	yu
he	nuy; nuydh	makrem	em
she	na; nadh	neur	em
we (you & I)	ngoeba; ngaba (M & K)	eaka	yumtu
we (we two, but not you)	ngalbe; ngalbay (M & K)	mimi	mitu
we (we & you)	ngalpa	mimi	yumpla
we (they & I, but not you)	ngoey	mimi	mipla
you (two) pl	ngipel; nipel (M & K)	kiki	yutu
you pl	ngitha; nitha (M & K)	kikiama	yupla
they (two)	palay	gairle	dhemtu
they	thana	gairle	dhempla

Greetings & civilities

KALA LAGAW YA

How are you?	**Ngi midh?** (KKY)
	Ni midhikidh? (M & K)
Fine.	**Balabayginga.** (KKY)
	Matha mina. (M & K)
Have you eaten?	**Ngi aydu purathima a?** (KKY)
	Ni aydun purthema a? (M)
	Ni aydun purthema? (K)
I've eaten already.	**Ngath aygud mu-asin.** (KKY)
	Ngaw/Nguzu aygud mina-asin. m/f (M & K)
I haven't eaten yet.	**Ngay aydu purthayginga.** (KKY)
	Ngaw/Nguzu ayngu purthayginga. m/f (M & K)
Come inside the house!	**Aya, ngapa lagiya muyari!** (KKY)
	Aye, ngapa mudhiya uth! (M & K)
Thank you.	**Eso.** (KKY, M & K)
Very good.	**Mina boelbayginga.** (KKY)
	Matha mina. (M & K)

MERIAM MIR

How are you?	**Nako manali?**
Fine.	**Sikakanali.**
Have you eaten?	**Aka ma lewer erwe?**
I've eaten already.	**Kai emethu lewer erwe?**
I haven't eaten yet.	**Ka nole lewer erwe?**
Come inside the house!	**Ma thaba bau mithem!**
Thank you.	**Eswau.**
Very good.	**Dhebe kaine.**

TORRES STRAIT BROKEN

How are you?	**Wis wei (yu)?**
Fine.	**Orait.**
Have you eaten?	**U bi kaikai?**

I've eaten already. ***Ai bi pinis kaikai.***
I haven't eaten yet. ***Ai no bi kaikai.***
Come inside the house! ***Kam insaid hous!***
Thank you. ***Eso po yu.***
Very good. ***Prapa gud.***

People & animals

	Kala Lagaw Ya	Meriam Mir	TSB
baby	mapeth (KKY) moekaz (M) moegikaz (K)	kebi werem	beibi
cat	pusi	pusi	pusi
dog	umay	omai	dog
friend	igalayg (KKY) thubudh (M & K)	kimeg	pren
man	gargaz (KKY) garka (M & K)	kimiar	man
old man	kulba thathi (KKY) koey kaz (M & K)	au le	ol man
old woman	kulba apu(KKY) koey kaz (M & K)	au kosker	ol oman
person	mabayg	le	man
rat	makas	mukeis	rat
snake	thabu (KKY) thab (M & K)	tabo	sneik
woman	yoepkaz (KKY) ipika (M & K)	kosker	oman

Useful words & phrases

	Kala Lagaw Ya	Meriam Mir	TSB
Yes.	Wa.	Baru.	Wa.
No.	Lawnga.	Nole.	No.
Welcome.	Sew ngapa.	Maiem.	Maiem.
Goodbye.	Yawa. (KKY)	Yawo.	Siyu; Yawo.
church	Yoewth (KKY) Maygi mudh (M & K)	Zogo metha Meb	Sos mun
drum	burubur (KKY) warup (M & K)	Warup	dram
God	Augadh (KKY, M & K)	Ople	Oli Gos
Holy Spirit	Maygi mari (KKY) Maygi mar (M & K)	Lamar zogo	—
moon	moelpal (KKY) kisay (M & K)	—	—
priest	misnare (KKY & K) niyay kaz (M)	Bab	pris

Directions & the countryside

	Kala Lagaw Ya	Meriam Mir	TSB
above	gimal	kotho	antap
behind	kalanu	keubu	biyain
below	apal	sep	andanith
beside	pasinu	meke	klustun
fire	muy	ur	paya
hill	pad	paser	il
in front	parunu	kikem	prant

>

<	Kala Lagaw Ya	Meriam Mir	TSB
left side	boedhadhoegam	kemer pek	lep said
path	yabugud	kebi gab	rod
right	gethadoegam	pedike	rait
river	koesa	-riba	—
rock	kula	bakir	ston
smoke	thu	kemur	smok
sun	goeygalim	san	—
tree	puy	lu	tri

D

H

Index

don't just stand there, say something!

To see the full range of our language products, go to:

lonelyplanet.com

What kind of traveller are you?

A. You're eating chicken for dinner *again* because it's the only word you know.

B. When no one understands what you say, you step closer and shout louder.

C. When the barman doesn't understand your order, you point frantically at the beer.

D. You're surrounded by locals, swapping jokes, email addresses and experiences – other travellers want to borrow your phrasebook or audio guide.

If you answered A, B, or C, you NEED Lonely Planet's language products ...

- **Lonely Planet Phrasebooks** – for every phrase you need in every language you want
- **Lonely Planet Language & Culture** – get behind the scenes of English as it's spoken around the world – learn and laugh
- **Lonely Planet Fast Talk & Fast Talk Audio** – essential phrases for short trips and weekends away – read, listen and talk like a local
- **Lonely Planet Small Talk** – 10 essential languages for city breaks
- **Lonely Planet Real Talk** – downloadable language audio guides from lonelyplanet.com to your MP3 player

... and this is why

- **Talk to everyone everywhere**
  Over 120 languages, more than any other publisher

- **The right words at the right time**
  Quick-reference colour sections, two-way dictionary, easy pronunciation, every possible subject – and audio to support it

Lonely Planet Offices

Australia
90 Maribyrnong St, Footscray,
Victoria 3011
☎ 03 8379 8000
fax 03 8379 8111
✉ talk2us@lonelyplanet.com.au

USA
150 Linden St, Oakland,
CA 94607
☎ 510 893 8555
fax 510 893 8572
✉ info@lonelyplanet.com

UK
72-82 Rosebery Ave,
London EC1R 4RW
☎ 020 7841 9000
fax 020 7841 9001
✉ go@lonelyplanet.co.uk

lonelyplanet.com